WRITER: **MATT FRACTION**

FANTASTIC FOUR #1-3

PENCILER: **MARK BAGLEY**
INKER: **MARK FARMER** WITH **MARK MORALES** (#2)
COLORIST: **PAUL MOUNTS** WITH **WIL QUINTANA** (#2)
COVER ARTISTS: **MARK BAGLEY**, **MARK FARMER** & **PAUL MOUNTS**

FF #1-3 AND MATERIAL FROM *MARVEL NOW! POINT ONE #1*

ARTIST: **MICHAEL ALLRED**
COLOR ARTIST: **LAURA ALLRED**
COVER ARTISTS: **MICHAEL** & **LAURA ALLRED**

LETTERER: **VC'S CLAYTON COWLES**
ASSISTANT EDITOR: **JAKE THOMAS**
EDITORS: **TOM BREVOORT** WITH **LAUREN SANKOVITCH**

COLLECTION EDITOR
CORY LEVINE
ASSISTANT EDITORS
ALEX STARBUCK & **NELSON RIBEIRO**
EDITORS, SPECIAL PROJECTS
JENNIFER GRÜNWALD & **MARK D. BEAZLEY**
SENIOR EDITOR, SPECIAL PROJECTS
JEFF YOUNGQUIST
SVP OF PRINT & DIGITAL PUBLISHING SALES
DAVID GABRIEL
BOOK DESIGN
JEFF POWELL & **CORY LEVINE**
EDITOR IN CHIEF
AXEL ALONSO
CHIEF CREATIVE OFFICER
JOE QUESADA
PUBLISHER
DAN BUCKLEY
EXECUTIVE PRODUCER
ALAN FINE

FANTASTIC FOUR VOL. 1: NEW DEPARTURE, NEW ARRIVALS. Contains material originally published in magazine form as FANTASTIC FOUR #1-3, FF #1-3 and MARVEL NOW! POINT ONE #1. First printing 2013. ISBN# 978-0-7851-6659-7. Published by MARVEL WORLDWIDE, INC., a subsidiary of MARVEL ENTERTAINMENT, LLC. OFFICE OF PUBLICATION: 135 West 50th Street, New York, NY 10020. **Printed in the U.S.A.** ALAN FINE, EVP - Office of the President, Marvel Worldwide, Inc. and EVP & CMO Marvel Characters B.V.; DAN BUCKLEY, Publisher & President - Print, Animation & Digital Divisions; JOE QUESADA, Chief Creative Officer; TOM BREVOORT, SVP of Publishing; DAVID BOGART, SVP of Operations & Procurement, Publishing; RUWAN JAYATILLEKE, SVP & Associate Publisher, Publishing; C.B. CEBULSKI, SVP of Creator & Content Development; DAVID GABRIEL, SVP of Print & Digital Publishing Sales; JIM O'KEEFE, VP of Operations & Logistics; DAN CARR, Executive Director of Publishing Technology; SUSAN CRESPI, Editorial Operations Manager; ALEX MORALES, Publishing Operations Manager; STAN LEE, Chairman Emeritus. For information regarding advertising in Marvel Comics or on Marvel.com, please contact Niza Disla, Director of Marvel Partnerships, at ndisla@marvel.com. For Marvel subscription inquiries, please call 800-217-9158. **Manufactured between 2/14/2013 and 3/9/2013 by QUAD/GRAPHICS, VERSAILLES, KY, USA.**

10 9 8 7 6 5 4 3 2 1

MARVEL NOW! POINT ONE #1

ANT-MAN
HEY, KIDS, IT'S
HEY, LOOK.
IT'S ART.
L.H.O.O.Q.
IT'S...
WHY'D YOU PUT A MUSTACHE ON THE MONA LISA?
I DIDN'T. A GUY NAMED DUCHAMP DID.
SEE, HE WAS, UH, I GUESS HE WAS TRYING TO SAY SOMETHING ABOUT ART AND MONEY AND STUFF.
SAY SOMETHING LIKE WHAT?
LIKE, IT WAS ART BECAUSE HE SAID IT WAS ART, AND THAT MAYBE ART SHOULDN'T TAKE ITSELF SO SERIOUSLY ALL THE TIME.
MAYBE ART WAS WHATEVER ANYBODY SAYS IT IS, AND SOMETIMES IT'S SILLY.
AND SOMETIMES SILLY IS OKAY TOO.
UM. FOUND IT?
WHERE DID YOU GET IT?
I LIKE IT.
YEAH. SILLY'S NOT SO BAD SOMETIMES.
HEY DID YOU WRITE THAT?
WE'RE LEARNING CURSIVE.
DO YOU LIKE IT?
I love you Daddy

THEN DOCTOR DOOM KILLED CASSIE.
...PERHAPS THEY'LL EVEN SAVE ME THE TROUBLE OF HAVING TO **KILL YOU.**
HE KILLED MY DAUGHTER.
VICTOR VON DOOM KILLED MY DAUGHTER.
IT TOOK ME **SIX WEEKS** TO EVEN BE ABLE TO **SAY THAT** OUT LOUD WITHOUT LOSING MY MIND.

TOOK ME NINETEEN TO BE READY TO GET BACK TO WORK.
MY NAME IS SCOTT LANG. I USED TO TRADE AS ANT-MAN.
NOW I'M A MIDDLE AGED EX-CON WITH A BLACK HOLE AT THE HEART OF HIS WORLD.
A HOLE CALLED DOOM.
I'VE NEVER BEEN A GUY PARTICULARLY COMPELLED BY REVENGE, I DON'T THINK.
AND YET HERE I AM.
DOOM THE ART OF LATVERIA
SNEAKING IN TO A LATVERIAN ART SHOW TO DO A LITTLE DAMAGE.
BECAUSE WHAT WAS THE ALTERNATIVE?
DRINKING DINNER ALONE AGAIN? CRYING IN THE SHOWER?
NO. I'M ALL DONE WITH THAT. I WANT A LITTLE PAYBACK. I'M ONLY HUMAN.
IF YOU WANT A SUPER HERO, GO READ ANOTHER COMIC.

MEET THE DEMODEX. AN EYELASH MITE.
JUST ONE OF THE MANY COMPLETELY HORRIFYING MICROSCOPIC MONSTERS THAT LIVE ON YOU AND IN YOU AT ALL TIMES.
THEY'RE CLASSIFIED AS COMMENSALS. THEY DON'T HURT YOU, YOU DON'T HURT THEM, THEY GET SOMETHING OUT OF THE DEAL, AND YOU GET TINY BUGS ON YOUR FACE.
VOORT
HARMLESS. SHOULD BE HARMLESS.
THIS GUY APPARENTLY DOESN'T READ WIKIPEDIA LIKE I DO.
TZZZK!
C'MON C'MON C'MON COME ON, SCOTT--
HOPE I DIDN'T UPSCALE TOO QUICKLY, SOMETIMES THERE ARE--

--CONSEQUENCES--
YOU OKAY, DARLA? BECAUSE THAT IS A RIDICULOUS FACE TO MAKE IN PUBLIC WITH ALL THESE CAMERAS AROUND.
YEAH, JUST--
--OH GOD, DID ANYBODY SEE?
AAAAA
GOOD NEWS/ BAD NEWS--
GOOD NEWS IS THE MICROMAG RIG TOTALLY WORKS IN SITUATIONS LIKE THIS.
BAD NEWS IS THE EMBASSY IS LACED WITH THE LATEST AND GREATEST IN LATVERIAN NANOSECURITY.
HUNTER/KILLER DRONES MEANT TO LOOK FOR WEE TINY JERKS LIKE ME THAT'VE TRIED TO SNEAK IN...

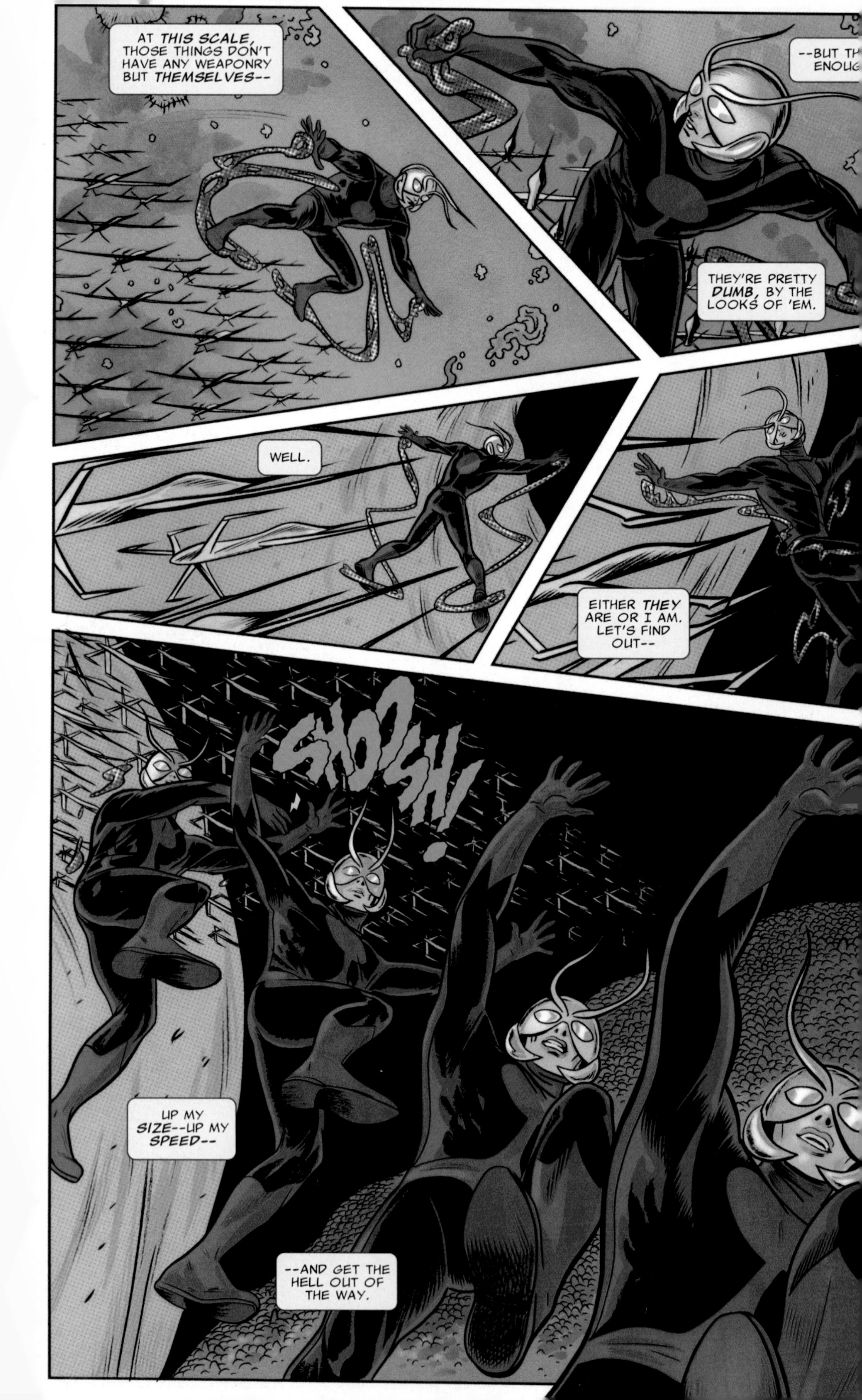
AT THIS SCALE, THOSE THINGS DON'T HAVE ANY WEAPONRY BUT THEMSELVES--
--BUT TH ENOUG
THEY'RE PRETTY DUMB, BY THE LOOKS OF 'EM.
WELL.
EITHER THEY ARE OR I AM. LET'S FIND OUT--
SHOOSH!
UP MY SIZE--UP MY SPEED--
--AND GET THE HELL OUT OF THE WAY.

TA-DAAAAA.
yyhhhaaawww.
THIS IS BORING. CAN WE GO?
WHEN CAN WE GO?
THE PAPARAZZI GOT US COMING IN, SO--YEAH, I GUESS SO.
BESIDES, IT KINDA FEELS LIKE WE'VE SEEN ALL THE GOOD STUFF ALREADY.
I LAY MY COURSE IN AND JUST TRY TO KEEP FROM CRASHING INTO RANDOM SPORES OR MOLECULES OF PERFUME IN THE AIR.
AT MY SIZE, IT'S GOING TO TAKE ALL NIGHT TO GET TO WHERE I'M GOING...
...AND I STILL HAVE TO TAKE CARE OF THINGS ONCE I GET THERE...

POLICE LINE - DO NOT CROSS
WHAT? I'M ONLY HUMAN.
EVERYBODY'S GOTTA START SOMEWHERE.
LOOK
Doom AS SEEN BY Doom
CRIME SCENE DO NOT CROSS
CRIME SCENE DO NOT CROSS
ENTER - CRIME SCENE - DO
FF

FANTASTIC FOUR #1 — "UNSTABLE"

ONE YEAR FROM NOW:
AR

THE FANTASTIC FOUR

A brilliant scientist—his best friend—the woman he loves—and her fiery-tempered kid brother! Together, they braved the unknown terrors of outer space and were changed by cosmic rays into something more than merely human! MR. FANTASTIC! THE THING! THE INVISIBLE WOMAN! THE HUMAN TORCH! Now they are the FANTASTIC FOUR, and the world will never be the same again!

Looking ever forward, Mr. Fantastic created The Future Foundation, designed to nurture the brightest young minds, including their children Franklin and Valeria, towards creating a better tomorrow. However, the call of progress is also the call of adventure, and discovery waits for no man, woman, child, or Thing. The Future is Now. And it is Fantastic.

Valeria Richards
Reed Richards • Mr. Fantastic
Franklin Richards
Sue Storm Richards • Invisible Woman
Ben Grimm • The Thing
Johnny Storm • The Human Torch

NOW:
MOMMMMAAAA!!
OH MAN.
OH MAN.
S'JUST A DREAM.
OH MAN.
MOMMA...?
FRANKLIN...
MOMMA...!
OH...
...THE MOMBOTS...
FRANKLIN
THERE THERE
FRANKLIN
FRANKLIN
THERE THERE
I WANT MY MOM.
I WANT MY MOMMMMMM!!

TWO-POINT-SIX-SIX MILLION YEARS BEFORE NOW, THE MOMENT WHEN EVERYTHING WENT WRONG:
AGHHH!
REED!
WHATTA REVOLTIN' DEVELOPMENT.
AHHHH--
--IT'S OKAY, IT'S OKAY--
REED, YOUR ARM-- HOW IS THAT EVEN POSSIBLE?
I PROMISE YOU I'LL LOOK INTO IT JUST AS SOON AS IT STOPS HURTING, SUSAN...

BBWOOOAAARRR!!
...AND WE'RE NOT IN DANGER OF BEING EATEN...
ANY TIME NOW, STRETCH!
ANY TIME.
JUST WANT TO POINT OUT AGAIN HOW THIS IS NOT MY FAULT--
SHUT UP, JOHNNY!
TK TK TK
ALMOST... ALMOST--
TORCH, IF I GOTTA PUNCH OUR WAY OUTTA SOME DINOSAUR'S GUTS TONIGHT, I SW--

4 THE BAXTER BUILDING. BREAKFAST NOOK.
THE GLORIOUS RETURN OF THE BEN!
ALL OF MY BREAKFAST PRAYERS HAVE BEEN ANSWERED!
MOM!
MY MUFFINS!
AR
DON'T GO AWAY AGAIN. OKAY? DON'T GO--
FRANKLIN-- BABY--
--BABY, IT'S OKAY, IT'S--
BAD DREAMS, DAD.
PICKED A GREAT TIME TO GO DORKING AROUND THE CRETACEOUS THERE, DAD.

WELL...
UNTIL WE GET THE NEW TABLE DELIVERED, THIS WILL HAVE TO DO...
DIG IN, EVERYBODY.
IT'S A MUTINY! A MUTINY, I TELL YA--!
SEIZE THE DUMPLINGS, BROTHERS!
FRANKLIN, SWEETIE, YOU NEED TO EAT.
S'OKAY, MOM. I'M NOT HUNGRY.
BABY, I'M WORRIED ABOUT YOU.
I JUST DON'T WANNA GO INTO SPACE, OKAY?
SPACE, WHAT ARE YOU--
REED, HONEY, I--
EARTH TO REED...
I KNOW THAT LOOK...

4 THE THINK TANK.

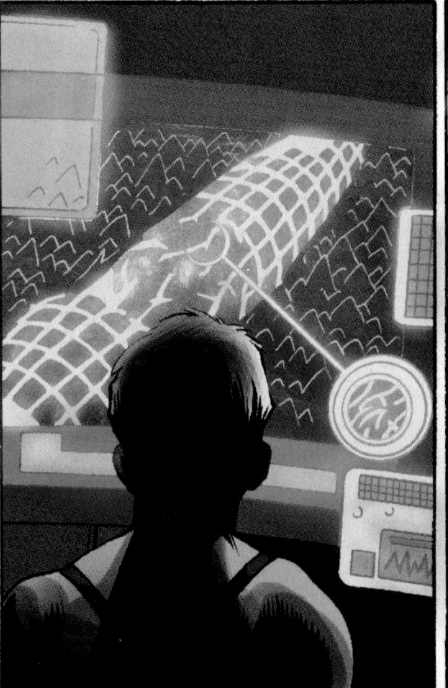

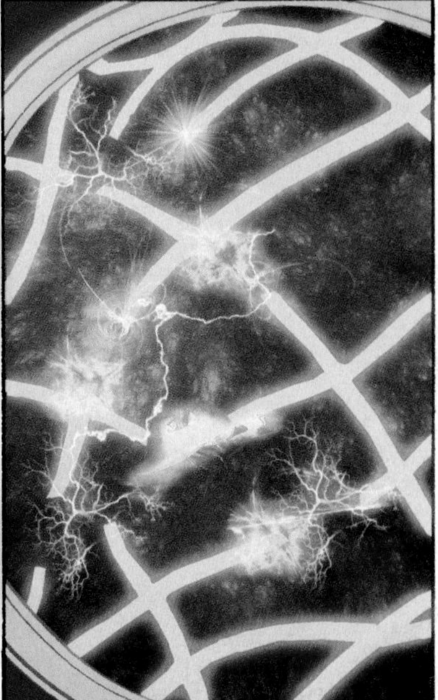

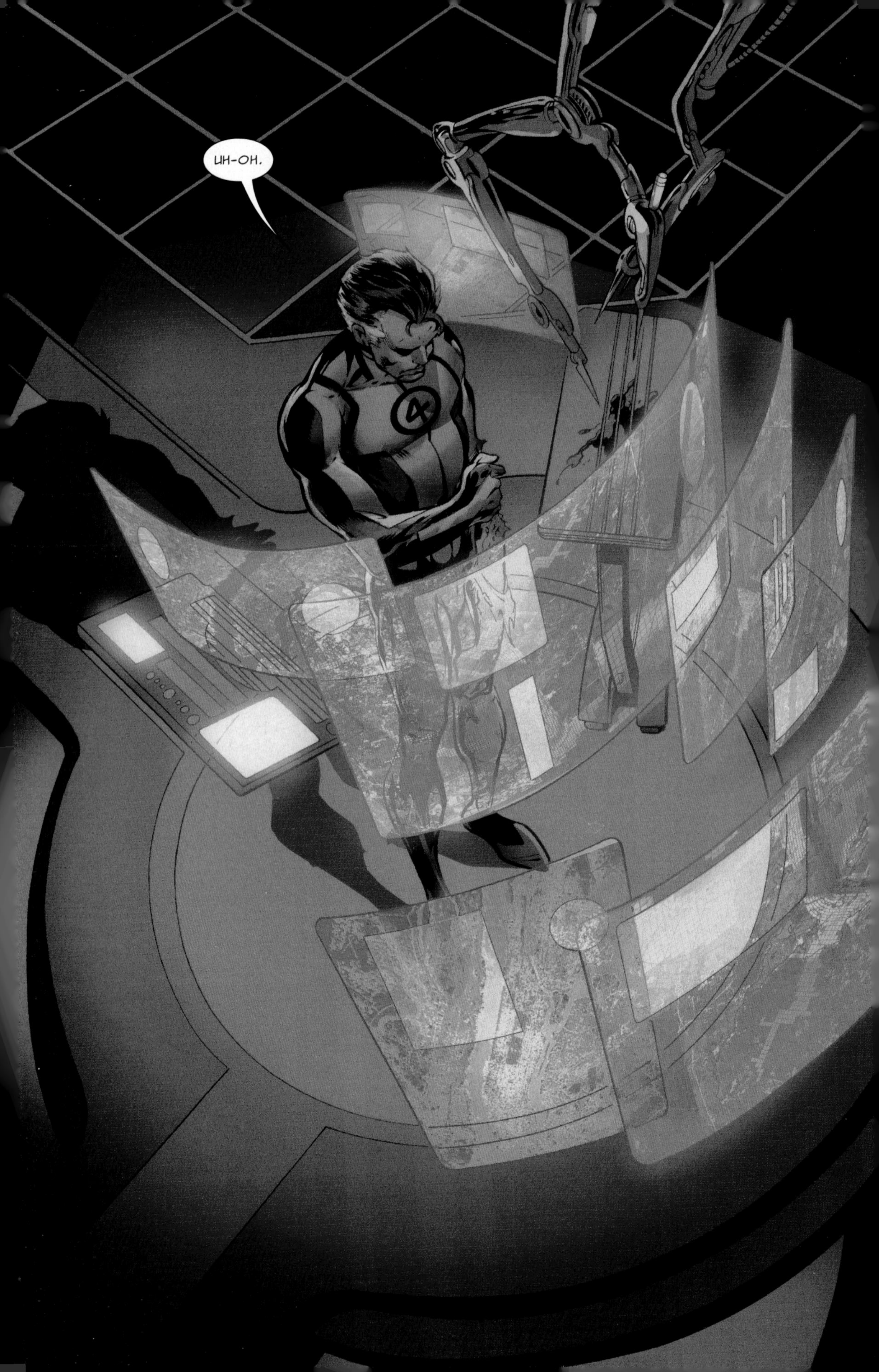
UH-OH.

YOU'RE MAD AT ME.
I'M NOT MAD.
PIZZAZZ
MS. THING DARLA DEERING ON LIVING THE DREAM!
AR
YOU'VE BEEN TALKING ABOUT YOUR CAR SINCE YOU PICKED ME UP.
MOTORCYCLE.
YOU HAVEN'T, LIKE, ASKED ME A SINGLE THING.
YOU'RE JUST-- TALKING.
LOOK, BABY, I DON'T WANT TO FIGHT, I JUST--
I'M NERVOUS.
I WANT TO MAKE THESE LAST FEW MONTHS UP TO YOU IS ALL. YOU SAID WE CAN NEVER GO OUT WITHOUT A DOZEN GUYS TRYING TO TAKE YOUR PICTURE OR MINE...
...OR THAT WE CAN NEVER EAT IN PEACE...
WELL, JACQUES HERE OWED ME FOR SAVING HIS PLACE DURING THE LAST NEW-YORK-GETS-LEVELLED EVENT...
'ALLO.
HE'S GREAT.
ITALIAN, PROBABLY.
ANYWAY, LOOK, THINGS HAVE BEEN NUTS LATELY, AND I JUST WANTED TO MAKE A SPECIAL NIGHT FOR JUST US.
I KNOW "SORRY" DOESN'T BUY THE TIME BACK OR HELP YOU UNWORRY ABOUT ME WHEN I WAS OFF BEING DEAD OR A SUPER HERO OR...
...BABY, THIS IS ME NOW. JOHNNY STORM. NOT THE HUMAN TORCH OR THE--
--DARLA, I BROUGHT YOU ALL THE WAY OUT HERE TO THE NEGATIVE ZONE TONIGHT SO I COULD TELL YOU THAT I...
...SEE, DARLA, I DON'T JUST LIKE YOU, I...

OHHH...
OH.
I LIKE YOU LIKE YOU, DARLS. YOU'RE, LIKE, SO SUPER-HOT. AND TOTALLY SWEET, AND I DON'T CARE WHAT YOUR MOM LOOKS LIKE, YOU'RE NOT GONNA LOOK LIKE HER WHEN YOU GET OLD.
SO THAT'S MY ACTUAL NUMBER THERE. DIRECT LINE. YOU FEEL ME? ANY TIME YOU NEED A LITTLE HEAT...
(352) 555-6366
YOU JUST CALL.
WELL, WELL. JOHNNY STORM.
YOU SURE KNOW HOW TO MAKE A GIRL FEEL SPECIAL.

4 YANCY STREET.
GRIMM YOUTH CENTER
YOU KNOW THE RULES.
HIT FIRST, FIGHT HARD, FIRST ONE THAT CAN'T GET UP LOSES.
DO IT FOR THE STREET.
FIGHT CLUB
GET SOME!!
FIGHT!
ggfffhhh
RRAAH!
HEY!

WHAT IN THE WORLD D'YOU THINK YOU'RE DOIN' HERE?
I ASKED YOU A QUESTION, DUMMIES.
ANSWER ME!
WHAT'S IT LOOK LIKE, DUMMY?
WE'RE FIGHTIN'.
WHO YOU CALLIN' DUMMY, DUMMY? YOU'R THE DUMMY WHAT BROK INTA MY COMMUNITY CENTER AND--
WHOA, DUMMY, IT'S A "COMMUNITY CENTER" FOR THE COMMUNITY, YA BIG DUMB SON OF A DUMB--
CHEESE IT, YANCY STREET!
SEE YA LATER, SELL-OUT DUMMY!
HEYHEYHEY!
...
DUMMIES.

NCY S†R33† GΔNG vs DUMMMY
NEW TOOB
YANCY STREET GANG. HATE THOSE GUYS.
4:00 / 5:00
Like
Share
508
YΔNCY S†R33† GΔNG vs DUMMMY
NEW TOOB
WHAT THE HEY?
4:10 / 5:00
Like
Share
1,067
NCY S†R33† GΔNG vs DUMMMY
NEW TOOB
ZATTA... CAMERA?
4:20 / 5:00
Like
Share
8,694
YΔNCY S†R33† GΔNG vs DUMMMY
NEW TOOB
RUNNIN' TA THAT COMPUTER AN...
4:30 / 5:00
Like
Share
35,905
NCY S†R33† GΔNG vs DUMMMY
NEW TOOB
HELLO?
4:40 / 5:00
Like
Share
598,260
YΔNCY S†R33† GΔNG vs DUMMMY
NEW TOOB
AR
I'M GONNA GET YOU, YANCY STREET DUMMIES!
YOU HEAR ME? I'LL GET EVERY LAST ONE A' YOU DUM--
4:50 / 5:00
Like
Share
1,000,000

JOURNAL ENTRY. TIMESTAMP. Nth ENCRYPTION ON CLOSING, PLEASE.
FILE START:
THERE'S SOMETHING VERY WRONG WITH ME.
THE UNSTABLE MOLECULES THAT HAVE CREATED MY ELASTIC PHYSIOGNOMY SEEM TO HAVE REACHED SOME POINT OF CELLULAR ENTROPY.
THEY'RE BREAKING APART--I'M BREAKING APART, AT A MOLECULAR LEVEL. MY CONCERN IS THAT THE OTHERS ARE AFFECTED TOO-- OR WILL BE VERY SOON.
MY POWERS ARE DYING, AND THEY'RE TAKING ME WITH THEM.
ENTER THE SE
CLASSIFICATI
THIS MEASUR
UNCLASSIFIE
CONFIDENTIAL
SECRET - 'S'
TOP SECRET - 'T'
OTHER - 'O'
H.E.R.B.I.E., A QUESTION:
IS THERE ANYTHING IN THE KNOWN UNIVERSE THAT CAN REVERSE MOLECULAR DECAY OF THIS RATE, ON THIS SCALE?
NEGATIVE, SIR.
SO THAT JUST LEAVES THE UNKNOWN UNIVERSES THEN, HM?
CORRECT, SIR.
I WAS JOKING, H.E.R.B.I.E., I--
...UNKNOWN UNIVERSES...
H.E.R.B.I.E.-- NEW PROJECT FILE. OPEN.
NOTES ON THE REDESIGN AND RETROFITTING OF THE HYPER-DIMENSIONAL WARSHIP PESTILENCE...

BENTLEY RULES!!
FOUR MINUTES. THEY WERE ALONE FOUR MINUTES.
HOW IS THIS EVEN POSSIBLE?
GASP!
SIGH.
MY CIRCUS.

GOOD NIGHT, MRS. RICHARDS.
GOOD NIGHT, DRAGON MAN.
NO NO NO NO--
HEY SUZIE, HOW DO YOU DELETE THINGS OFFA DA INTERNET?
I HAVE NO IDEA, BEN. SORRY.

GOOD NIGHT HOUSE, GOOD NIGHT MOUSE...
GOOD NIGHT, BAXTER BUILDING.

HM.

HI, MOM.
CAN I, UM...
I WAS WONDERING, MAYBE I COULD SLEEP IN HERE TONIGHT?
nnzzrrk.
SUE.
SUE.
--HM? REED?
SUSAN, I'M SORRY FOR LEAVING THE DINNER TABLE SO ABRUPTLY EARLIER THIS EVENING.
IT WAS RUDE, AND I APOLOGIZE.
BUT I'VE HAD AN AMAZING IDEA...

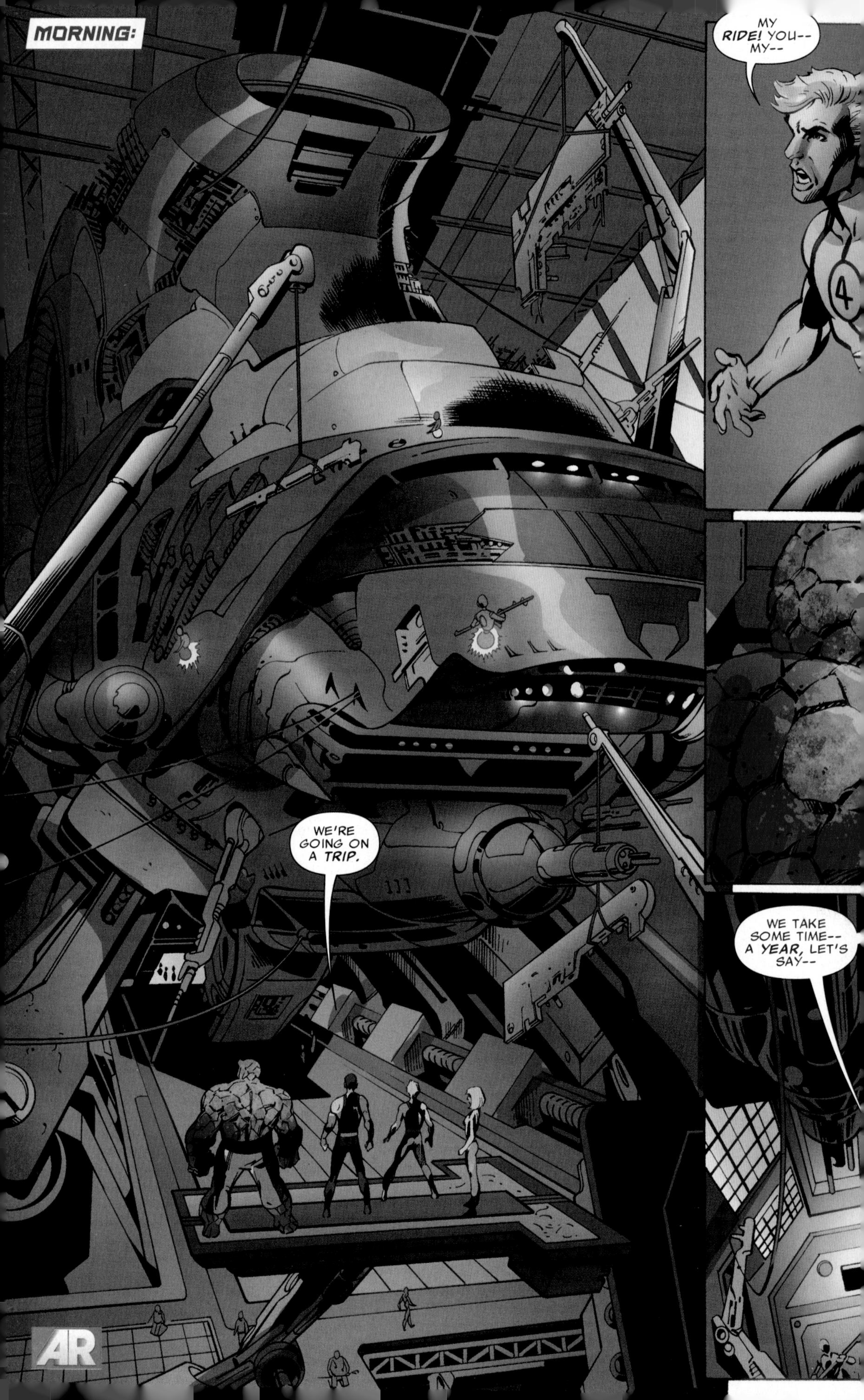
MORNING:
MY RIDE! YOU-- MY--
WE'RE GOING ON A TRIP.
WE TAKE SOME TIME-- A YEAR, LET'S SAY--
AR

REED, THE ESTILENCE WAS FLAGSHIP OF THE IGHT BRIGADE! IT WAS--
--DRY-DOCKED IN MIDTOWN MANHATTAN, JOHNNY.
AFTER WE STRIP THE GUNS OFF OF HER, WE'RE GOING TO TRANSFORM IT INTO THE GREATEST CLASSROOM EVER CONCEIVED.
SHE'LL TAKE US AND THE KIDS EVERYWHERE WE COULD POSSIBLY IMAGINE.
VAL SAID SOMETHING WHEN WE GOT HOME YESTERDAY, AND IT STUNG--
THE KIDS NEEDED US AND WE WERE GONE. I WAS GONE. FRANKLIN WAS UPSET AND...
AND I DON'T WANT TO BE GONE ANYMORE.
SO I WONDERED, WHY NOT TAKE THE KIDS WITH US? WHY NOT SHOW THEM WHAT WE SEE? SAFELY, OF COURSE. LESS ACTION, MORE ADVENTURE.
AGAIN, I JUST WANT TO POINT OUT THAT WAS NOT MY FAULT--
WE HAVE A SHIP MADE TO SAIL THROUGH SPACE AND TIME ITSELF IS MY POINT. SO THEN LET'S SAIL IT.
--AND WE EXPLORE TOGETHER LIKE THE STRONAUT FAMILY WE RE. WHAT ARE THE KIDS TUDYING? WHAT DO THEY WANT TO LEARN? LET'S GO SEE IT FIRST-HAND. LIVE IT.
WE'LL BUILD A CURRICULUM ON THE FLY. WE'LL GO WATCH THE BIG BANG AND THEN THE BIG CRUNCH. LET'S DINE WITH KINGS AND VISIT IMPOSSIBLE POSSIBILITIES.
AND THE BEST PART IS...
...IT'S A SPACE-TIME MACHINE. WE CAN RETURN MOMENTS AFTER WE LEAVE.
I JUST DON'T WANNA GO INTO SPACE, OKAY?
WHAT'S THE WORST THAT COULD HAPPEN?

"YEAR'S A LOTTA TIME THERE, STRETCH."
"OF COURSE. AND I RESPECT THAT. BUT REMEMBER--IT'S JUST A YEAR TO US. FOR EVERYONE HERE, IT'LL BE A FEW MOMENTS WE'RE AWAY."
"AND YOU'RE SURE THAT WILL WORK? EVERYONE WILL BE SAFE?"
"OH MY, NO. THE BIG BANG HAPPENED IN LESS THAN A SECOND. WE SHOULD CHOOSE TEMPORARY REPLACEMENTS."
"BUT IF WE'RE ONLY GONE A FEW MINUTES--"
THEN WE WILL ENSURE THE EARTH HAS A FOUR TO STAND FOR IT.
A MINUTE, A SECOND, A LIFETIME--WE DO NOT LEAVE THE EARTH UNPROTECTED.
REED, IS SUCH AN EXTENDED TRIP WISE? YOU GOT REALLY HURT YESTERDAY.
MAYBE WE SHOULD--
SUSAN.
I'M FINE.
TRUST ME.

FF #1 — "PARTS OF A HOLE"

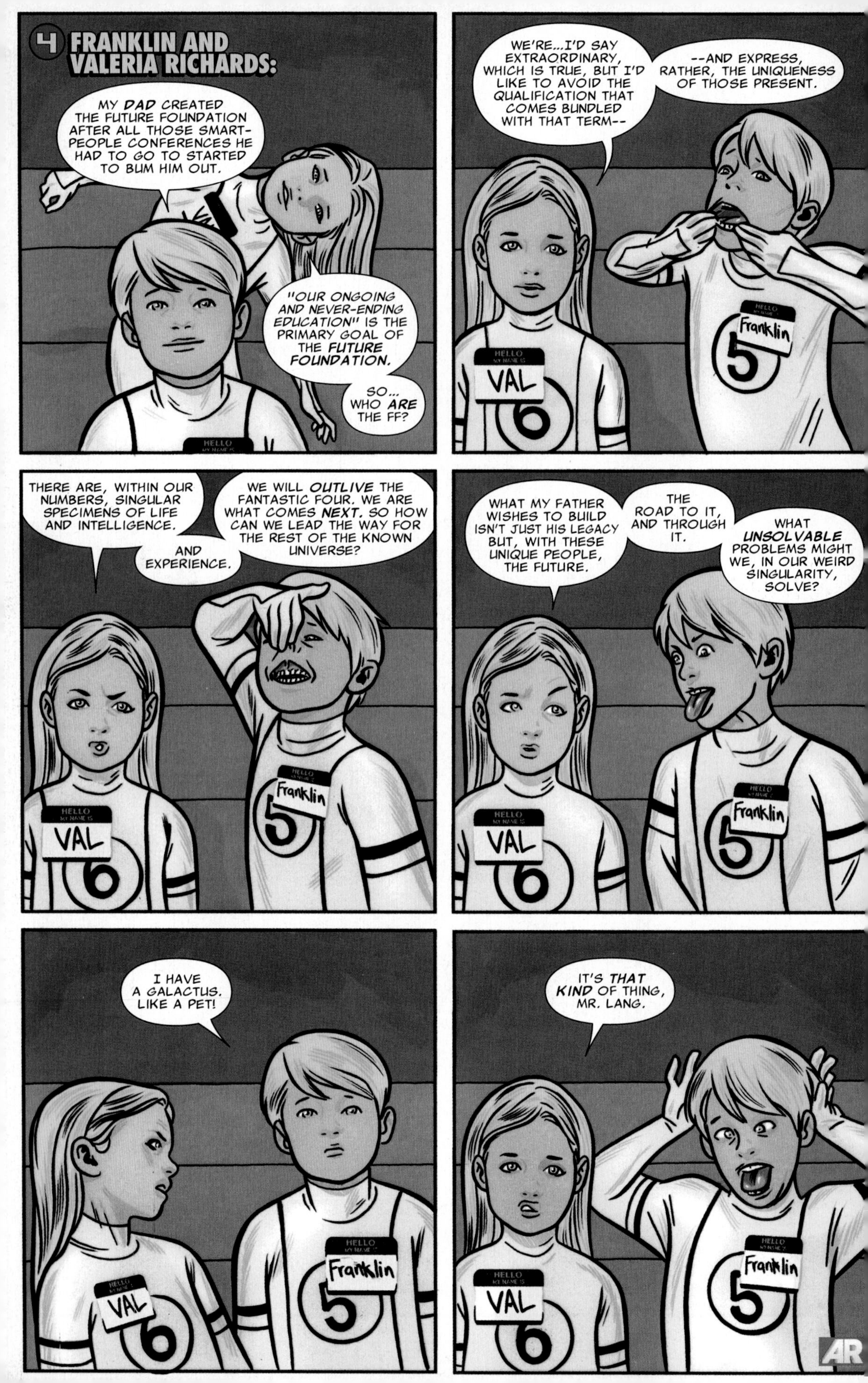
4 FRANKLIN AND VALERIA RICHARDS:
MY DAD CREATED THE FUTURE FOUNDATION AFTER ALL THOSE SMART-PEOPLE CONFERENCES HE HAD TO GO TO STARTED TO BUM HIM OUT.
"OUR ONGOING AND NEVER-ENDING EDUCATION" IS THE PRIMARY GOAL OF THE FUTURE FOUNDATION.
SO... WHO ARE THE FF?
HELLO MY NAME IS
WE'RE...I'D SAY EXTRAORDINARY, WHICH IS TRUE, BUT I'D LIKE TO AVOID THE QUALIFICATION THAT COMES BUNDLED WITH THAT TERM--
--AND EXPRESS, RATHER, THE UNIQUENESS OF THOSE PRESENT.
HELLO MY NAME IS VAL
HELLO MY NAME IS Franklin
THERE ARE, WITHIN OUR NUMBERS, SINGULAR SPECIMENS OF LIFE AND INTELLIGENCE.
AND EXPERIENCE.
WE WILL OUTLIVE THE FANTASTIC FOUR. WE ARE WHAT COMES NEXT. SO HOW CAN WE LEAD THE WAY FOR THE REST OF THE KNOWN UNIVERSE?
HELLO MY NAME IS VAL
Franklin
WHAT MY FATHER WISHES TO BUILD ISN'T JUST HIS LEGACY BUT, WITH THESE UNIQUE PEOPLE, THE FUTURE.
THE ROAD TO IT, AND THROUGH IT.
WHAT UNSOLVABLE PROBLEMS MIGHT WE, IN OUR WEIRD SINGULARITY, SOLVE?
HELLO MY NAME IS VAL
HELLO Franklin
I HAVE A GALACTUS. LIKE A PET!
HELLO VAL
HELLO MY NAME IS Franklin
IT'S THAT KIND OF THING, MR. LANG.
HELLO MY NAME IS VAL
HELLO Franklin
AR

4 SCOTT LANG AND REED RICHARDS:
IT'S JUST NOT COMING TOGETHER.
I HAVE ALL THESE PARTS AND I CAN'T QUITE GET IT ALL TOGETHER.
HMM...
WHAT IS IT YOU'RE TRYING TO MAKE HERE, EXACTLY?
SOMETHING THAT WORKS, ANYTHING THAT WORKS, SOMETHING OF USE, I DON'T KNOW...
AR

I DEVELOPED A KIND OF COIL I CAN NAVIGATE WHEN I GET SMALL.
SEEMED MORE PRACTICAL THAN TRYING TO RIDE A BUG OR CONTROL A DUST MOTE DESCENT...
THINKING THIS SMALL IS ONE THING. ENGINEERING AT THIS SIZE IS JUST--
--FORGET ABOUT IT.
I TRIED TAKING IT APART TO FIX IT, BUT I THINK I JUST MADE IT WORSE...
INDEED. SAY, SCOTT...
I'VE COME HERE WITH...
WELL, RATHER A JOB OFFER.
BUT I WANTED TO SEE HOW YOU'RE DOING, FIRST.
I love you Daddy
YOU KNOW.
IN THE WAKE OF... AH...
WELL.
ALL OF THAT UNPLEASANTNESS.
AR

LET'S SEE. HOW AM I DOING? HOW AM I DOING?
I AM DOING UNPLEASANTLY, REED.
I LOST MY DAUGHTER, MAN.
I LOST EVERYTHING IN THIS "UNPLEASANTNESS." THAT'S HOW I'M DOING.
YES, WELL. SCOTT, I'M--I DON'T KNOW HOW TO TALK ABOUT THINGS LIKE THIS, AND I'M SORRY, SO LET ME SIMPLY CUT TO THE CHASE AND THEN GET OUT OF YOUR HAIR.
I'M GOING AWAY. THE FANTASTIC FOUR AS YOU KNOW IT IS. WE'RE TAKING THE...
WE'RE TAKING A TRIP.
I'M LEAVING WITH MY FAMILY, LEAVING EARTH, LEAVING RECOGNIZABLE TIME AND SPACE.
I'VE WORKED IT OUT WHERE WE'LL ONLY BE GONE FOUR MINUTES TO YOU HERE, BUT JUST IN CASE...WE'VE DECIDED TO FIND REPLACEMENTS.
JUST IN CASE.
SO I'M ASKING-- FOR FOUR MINUTES-- WOULD ANT-MAN STAND IN MY PLACE AT THE HEAD OF THE FF?
WHAT?

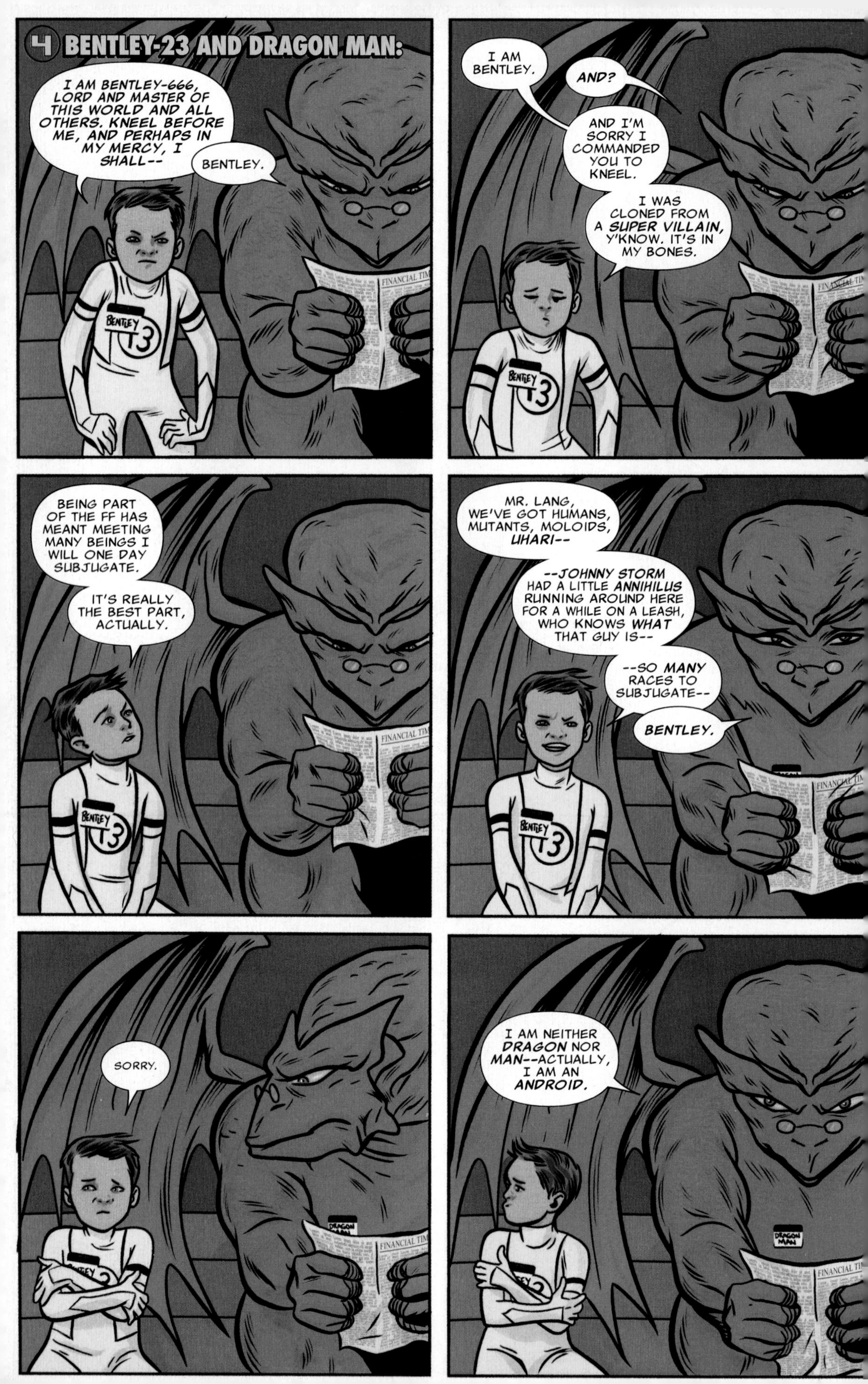
4 BENTLEY-23 AND DRAGON MAN:
I AM BENTLEY-666, LORD AND MASTER OF THIS WORLD AND ALL OTHERS. KNEEL BEFORE ME, AND PERHAPS IN MY MERCY, I SHALL--
BENTLEY.
BENTLEY 13
FINANCIAL TIMES
I AM BENTLEY.
AND?
AND I'M SORRY I COMMANDED YOU TO KNEEL.
I WAS CLONED FROM A SUPER VILLAIN, Y'KNOW. IT'S IN MY BONES.
BEING PART OF THE FF HAS MEANT MEETING MANY BEINGS I WILL ONE DAY SUBJUGATE.
IT'S REALLY THE BEST PART, ACTUALLY.
MR. LANG, WE'VE GOT HUMANS, MUTANTS, MOLOIDS, UHARI--
--JOHNNY STORM HAD A LITTLE ANNIHILUS RUNNING AROUND HERE FOR A WHILE ON A LEASH, WHO KNOWS WHAT THAT GUY IS--
--SO MANY RACES TO SUBJUGATE--
BENTLEY.
SORRY.
DRAGON MAN
I AM NEITHER DRAGON NOR MAN--ACTUALLY, I AM AN ANDROID.
DRAGON MAN

4 SUE STORM-RICHARDS AND MEDUSA:
SUSAN.
CRYSTAL.
WELCOME BACK TO ATTILAN.
MY.
CAN'T BEAT THE VIEW, CAN YOU?
AR

WITH BLACK BOLT HAVING BUSINESS BELOW, IT SEEMED LOGICAL TO POSITION ATTILAN...NEARBY.
SHE'S WAITING FOR YOU INSIDE.
HE OKAY?
LOCKJAW WAITS FOR HIS MASTER.
COME.
"MEDUSA WILL SEE YOU NOW..."
SUSAN OF THE STORM, QUEEN OF UHARI; THE QUEEN MEDUSA OF THE INHUMANS.
YOUR HIGHNESS. WELCOME BACK.
YOUR HIGHNESS.
I'VE COME WITH AN OFFER.

SPENDING TIME TOGETHER WILL BE GOOD FOR US.
THE CLOSE QUARTERS MIGHT BE A LITTLE MUCH, BUT A VACATION TOGETHER FEELS EXACTLY LIKE THE THING WE NEED.
I ENVY YOU. WHICH IS NOT AN EASY THING FOR ME TO ADMIT.
I FEEL SOMETIMES AS IF MY MARRIAGE IS UNDER SIEGE BY EVERYTHING THAT SURROUNDS US.
BLACK BOLT AND I, BOUND TOGETHER, THE HEART OF A STAR BURNING BRIGHTLY AGAINST ALL THE DARKNESS IN THE UNIVERSE.
WELL, YOU'RE A PARENT. YOU KNOW WHAT IT'S LIKE TO HAVE YOUR HEART RUNNING AROUND OUTSIDE OF YOUR BODY ALL THE TIME.
AND ONCE YOU HAVE KIDS--
MM.
OURS HAS...
HE HAS NEEDS. MORE THAN MOST.
AND WE BROUGHT HIM--
--WE CHOSE TO BRING HIM--
--INTO OUR WORLD OF POLITICS, WAR, MURDER, MADNESS...
SOMETIMES, IT MAKES ME WANT TO RUN.
AND NEVER COME BACK.
TINK
SO THEN, WHAT IS THIS OFFER OF WHICH YOU SPEAK?

4
TONG, KORR, TURG AND MIK:
TURG
THE FUTURE FOUNDATION DOES MANY THINGS. MOST IMPORTANT IS TO SERVE THE BEN.
MIK
TONG
KORR
ALL THINGS ARE TO SERVE THE BEN.
SOME THINGS MORE THAN OTHER THINGS SERVE THE BEN.
THE BEN RESCUED US FROM THE FORGOTTEN CITY DEEP INSIDE THE DEEP INSIDES OF EVERYTHING.
LEFT FOR DEAD, WE WERE.
THE BEN TOOK US FROM THE DARK TO THE LIGHT! TO THIS GREAT PLACE OF SILVER AND GLASS AND EXPLOSIONS!
NOW WE ARE OF MANY PLACES. WE HAVE SEEN MANY THINGS.
SPACE PLACES!
YES.
THE THINGS WE HAVE SEEN! THE WORLDS TO WHICH WE HAVE BEEN!
EVERYTHING. THE END OF EVERYTHING AND BEYOND EVERYTHING.
OUR COMPASS IS CURIOSITY. OUR DESTINATION IS THE INFINITE.
WHERE SHALL WE GO TODAY? OF WHAT SHALL WE CONCERN OURSELVES WITH?
AND WILL IT PLEASE THE BEN?
SHOES!
SHOES FOR THE BEN!

4 BEN GRIMM AND JENNIFER WALTERS:
C'MON, YA PANSY!
I THOUGHT YOU SAID YOU WANTED TA HIT SOMETHIN'!
PPFT.
THOK
RRRRRAAAHHH!!
SKRUNCH

STILL WITH US, BEN?
JEEZUM CROW, JENNIFER-- YOU REALLY ARE YOUR COUSIN'S COUSIN, Y'KNOW THAT?
I'M FEELING A LITTLE PENT UP THESE DAYS.
I WANT A LITTLE ACTION, YOU KNOW WHAT I MEAN?
THINK FAST!
D'AWWW, JEN--
SPLOOTCH
LOOK, SPEAKIN'A ACTION--
--WHATCHA DOIN' NEXT WEDNESDAY MORNING FROM, SAY, TEN TO ABOUT FOUR MINUTES AFTER?
OR MAYBE FOREVER?
I'M...
THAT'S INCREDIBLY SPECIFIC YET FRUSTRATINGLY VAGUE, BEN. WHAT DO YOU HAVE IN MIND?

WE'RE GOIN' ON A TRIP, JENNY-POO. THE FF, I MEAN.
AND WE'RE GONNA BE GONE--
--AND SISTER, I MEAN GONE-GONE!
TO US, IT'LL BE FOR ABOUT A YEAR, BUT TO YOU, IT'LL BE FOUR MINUTES. AN' REED WANTS US TO FIND... REPLACEMENTS, JUST IN CASE.
I'VE BEEN IN THE FANTASTIC FOUR BEFORE, BEN. I'VE REPLACED YOU IN THE FANTASTIC FOUR BEFORE.
SO WHY THE GRAVITAS THIS TIME, BUDDY?
BECAUSE IT'S US, JEN.
BECAUSE WHEN DOES ANYTHING GO THE WAY WE PLAN IT?
SO WHY ME?
BECAUSE, JENNY-JEN. EVEN THOUGH MY AUNT PETUNIA RAISED ME TO NEVER HIT NO DAMES...
...I DUNNO THAT I COULDA WHUPPED YA EVEN THENHEYHEY!!
AWW--
SPLITCH
FUNNY, SHULKIE.
REEEEEAL FUNNY.

4 VIL, WU AND ONOME:
ONOME 17
WU 14
VIL 15
AHH...
I'M RATHER NEW HERE MYSELF. I DON'T KNOW WHAT TO EXPECT YET, OR WHAT I *THINK*, OR...
I'VE NEVER MET ANY UHARI BEFORE.
I DON'T KNOW WHAT TO SAY.

4 JOHNNY STORM AND DARLA DEERING:
AAAHH!
JOHNNY...?
JEEZ, I JUST HAD THE WORST NIGHTMARE--
ONE OF THOSE--
--THOSE--
ARE YOU OKAY? IT WAS JUST A BAD DREAM...
NO, NO, I'M WORRIED I FORGOT SOMETHING IMPORTANT.
AH-HA! HERE IT IS. HERE, TODAY ON MY CALENDAR IT SAYS...
OH.
"ASK SOMEBODY ABOUT THE THING." THAT'S NO HELP.
UM. DO YOU LIKE THE THING? Y'KNOW-- BEN GRIMM?
BIG, DUMB, ORANGE ROCK GUY, TALKS LIKE AN OLD-TIMEY MOVIE?
YEAH, SURE, HE'S ALRIGHT, I GUESS.
BUT NOT AS MUCH AS THE HUMAN TORCH, RIGHT?
WHAT? NO, OF COURSE NOT.
COOL. I HAVE ASKED SOMEBODY ABOUT THE THING. NOW LET'S GET BREAKFAST.

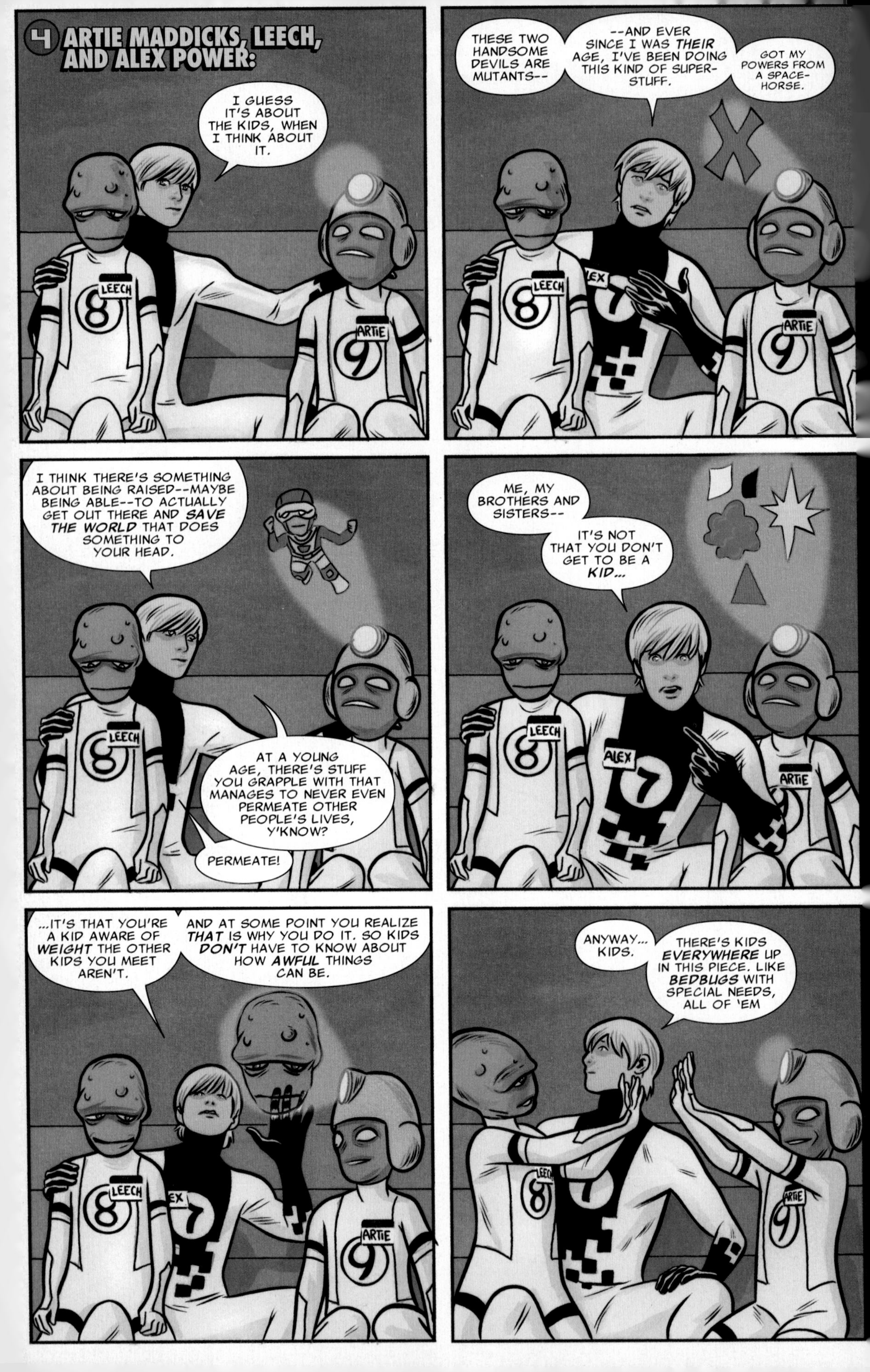
4 ARTIE MADDICKS, LEECH, AND ALEX POWER:
I GUESS IT'S ABOUT THE KIDS, WHEN I THINK ABOUT IT.
LEECH
ARTIE
THESE TWO HANDSOME DEVILS ARE MUTANTS--
--AND EVER SINCE I WAS THEIR AGE, I'VE BEEN DOING THIS KIND OF SUPER-STUFF.
GOT MY POWERS FROM A SPACE-HORSE.
I THINK THERE'S SOMETHING ABOUT BEING RAISED--MAYBE BEING ABLE--TO ACTUALLY GET OUT THERE AND SAVE THE WORLD THAT DOES SOMETHING TO YOUR HEAD.
AT A YOUNG AGE, THERE'S STUFF YOU GRAPPLE WITH THAT MANAGES TO NEVER EVEN PERMEATE OTHER PEOPLE'S LIVES, Y'KNOW?
PERMEATE!
ME, MY BROTHERS AND SISTERS--
IT'S NOT THAT YOU DON'T GET TO BE A KID...
ALEX
...IT'S THAT YOU'RE A KID AWARE OF WEIGHT THE OTHER KIDS YOU MEET AREN'T.
AND AT SOME POINT YOU REALIZE THAT IS WHY YOU DO IT. SO KIDS DON'T HAVE TO KNOW ABOUT HOW AWFUL THINGS CAN BE.
ANYWAY... KIDS.
THERE'S KIDS EVERYWHERE UP IN THIS PIECE. LIKE BEDBUGS WITH SPECIAL NEEDS, ALL OF 'EM

I ACCEPT.
I'M IN.
YAY!
NNNNNNNNO.
NO NO NO NO NO NO NO.
ABSOLUTELY NOT.
AR

4 THE FUTURE FOUNDATION:
NO.
I DON'T KNOW WHAT...
...WHAT THIS *IS*, REED. NO.
SCOTT, COME WITH ME, WON'T YOU?

SCOTT...
FF. YOU SAID "FF" AND I THOUGHT YOU MEANT FANTASTIC FOUR AND NOT--
I DID--
--AND NOT FUTURE FOUNDATION.
I DID. I MEANT BOTH.
SCOTT, LISTEN-- WE'RE TALKING ABOUT FOUR MINUTES.
I DON'T WANT ANYTHING TO DO WITH THOSE KIDS, REED!
I NEED YOU TO RESPECT THAT AND OPEN THAT DOOR AND LET ME GO HOME!
YOU'RE AN ADULT, SCOTT. YOU CAN COME AND GO AS YOU PLEASE.
I ASKED YOU FOR MANY REASONS. YOUR PAST HEROICS, YOUR MIND FOR SCIENCE AND--
--YES--
--YES, YOU ARE A FATHER LESS HIS CHILD. YOU ARE LIVING A NIGHTMARE THAT I LITERALLY CANNOT IMAGINE.
REED.
DID I PARSE MY LANGUAGE TO OBSCURE THE FACT YOU WOULD HAVE TO SPEND FOUR WHOLE MINUTES WITH THE CHILDREN OF THE FUTURE FOUNDATION? YES.
REED.
MOST FOLKS MIGHT THINK THESE ARE YOUR COOL SCIENCE SCREENSAVERS OR WHATEVER, BUT I KNOW CARCINOMIC GROWTH ON THE PICOSCALE WHEN I SEE IT.
WHO'S SICK?

ME. I AM. I'M SICK, SCOTT, AND I DON'T KNOW WITH WHAT PRECISELY OR HOW TO STOP IT.
THAT'S WHAT I BROUGHT YOU BACK HERE TO TALK ABOUT.
NO ONE KNOWS WHAT I'M ABOUT TO TELL YOU, SCOTT.
THIS TRIP I'M TAKING WITH MY FAMILY--THE EDUCATIONAL ASPECT IS JUST PRETENSE.
I'M LOOKING FOR A CURE, AND I KNOW FOR A FACT IT DOESN'T EXIST WITHIN OUR SPACETIME CONTINUUM.
I'M CONFIDENT WE'LL FIND IT-- I DON'T WANT ANYONE TO WORRY, HENCE THE SUBTERFUGE--AND I'M CONFIDENT WE'LL BE BACK THE MORNING WE LEAVE.
ALL THE SAME, I WILL NOT LEAVE THIS UNIVERSE UNPROTECTED.
SCOTT...THERE IS A ROOM FULL OF CHILDREN OUT THERE, UNIQUE AND SINGULAR, AND ALL OF THEM NEED THE FAMILY THE FF PROVIDES.
AM I GUILTY OF BRINGING YOU, A FATHER MISSING HIS DAUGHTER, TO THEM, IN HOPES YOU WOULD BE OF USE TO EACH OTHER? YES.
I'M NOT ASKING YOU TO ADOPT THEM, SCOTT. AND I KNOW NONE OF THEM CAN EVER REPLACE YOUR LOSS. BUT MAYBE...
MAYBE THERE'S A WAY YOU CAN ALL BE OF USE TO EACH OTHER IN MY ABSENCE.
REGARDLESS OF HOW LONG THAT LASTS.

GOOD MORNING. MY NAME IS SCOTT LANG.
I'VE BEEN A LOT OF THINGS IN MY LIFE.
I'M AN ENGINEER, A DESIGNER, A NANOTECH SPECIALIST, A TEACHER, A FATHER, A SUPER HERO...
AND IT SOUNDS LIKE, IN A FEW WEEKS, I'M GOING TO BE THE HEAD OF THE FUTURE FOUNDATION FOR A FEW MINUTES.
SO TELL ME.
IF YOU COULD DESIGN THE FUTURE FROM THE GROUND UP, WHAT WOULD IT LOOK LIKE?
AND MORE IMPORTANTLY--
WHAT IS THE FF? WHAT DOES IT MEAN TO YOU, THE YOUNG MINDS THAT MAKE UP THE PROGRAM?
FRANKLIN AND VAL--YOU START.
TEACH ME ABOUT THE FUTURE FOUNDATION.

FANTASTIC FOUR #2 — "VOYAGERS"

YANCY ST.
LISTEN UP, DUMMIES!
THIS IS MY LAST WILL AN' TESTAMENT AND I'M ONLY GONNA HOLLER IT ONCE!!
4

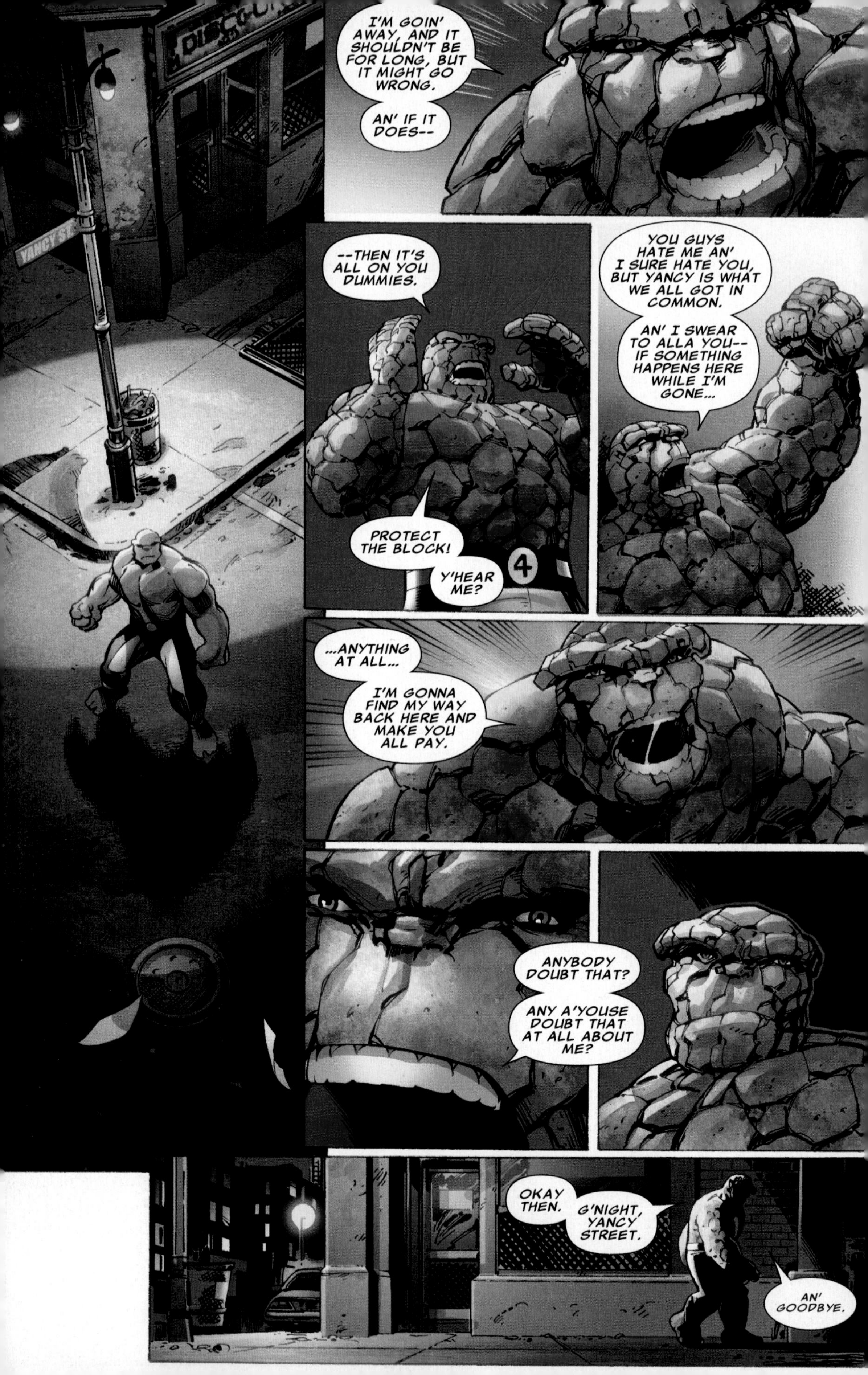
DISCOUNT
YANCY ST.
I'M GOIN' AWAY, AND IT SHOULDN'T BE FOR LONG, BUT IT MIGHT GO WRONG.
AN' IF IT DOES--
--THEN IT'S ALL ON YOU DUMMIES.
PROTECT THE BLOCK!
Y'HEAR ME?
YOU GUYS HATE ME AN' I SURE HATE YOU, BUT YANCY IS WHAT WE ALL GOT IN COMMON.
AN' I SWEAR TO ALLA YOU-- IF SOMETHING HAPPENS HERE WHILE I'M GONE...
...ANYTHING AT ALL...
I'M GONNA FIND MY WAY BACK HERE AND MAKE YOU ALL PAY.
ANYBODY DOUBT THAT?
ANY A'YOUSE DOUBT THAT AT ALL ABOUT ME?
OKAY THEN.
G'NIGHT, YANCY STREET.
AN' GOODBYE.

WHAT...
...REED... WHAT AM I LOOKING AT?
BECAUSE IT ACTUALLY LOOKS EVIL.
AR
IT'S WHAT HAPPENS TO UNSTABLE MOLECULES WHEN THEY TURN CANCEROUS, SCOTT.
IT'S UNLIKE ANYTHING I'VE EVER HAD TO FACE.
WELL, YOU'RE NOT ALONE IN THIS, REED.
DON'T FORGET THAT.

NO, NO, SCOTT, WE MUST KEEP THIS BETWEEN OURSELVES FOR NOW.
AT LEAST UNTIL I CAN GET MY HANDS AND HEAD AROUND THE PROBLEM. I DON'T KNOW HOW--
--OR IF--
--THERE'S A CURE. UNTIL I CAN DEFINE WHAT THE PROBLEM IS WITH PRECISION AND CONFIDENCE...
...I WOULD JUST CAUSE MY FAMILY TO PANIC AND WORRY.
YEAH, YEAH, GOD FORBID YOU HAVE A FAMIL THAT CARES ABOUT YOU.
YOU BROKE UP A LITTLE BI THERE, SCOTT- COME AGAIN?
I SAID, I'VE CAPTURED AT LEAST A PAIR OF CELLS ABOUT TO DIVIDE FOR YOU.
HOPEFULLY THEY'LL HELP YOU FIND SOME ANSWERS.
STAND-BY FOR RAPID UP-SIZING.
PLEASE, SCOTT. I NEED YOUR WORD.
ABSOLUTE SECRECY.
IF YOU SAY SO, REED.
IF YOU SAY SO.

KIDS, I'D LIKE YOU TO MEET MEDUSA, QUEEN OF THE INHUMANS.
MEDUSA, THIS IS THE FUTURE FOUNDATION. I THOUGHT IT MIGHT BE NICE TO HAVE A MORE INTIMATE INTRODUCTION THAN A CLASSROOM SETTING MAY ALLOW.
NO ONE IS BOWING.
THEY'RE NOT TOO BIG ON BOWING HERE, I DON'T THINK.
IN FAIRNESS, THEY DID MANAGE TO ALL HOLD STILL FOR MOST OF A MINUTE, SO...
YOUR MAJESTY!
OH, DEAR.

C'MON, BENJY-BOY...
...THOUGHT YOU SAID WE WOULD WORK OUT.
WELL, I DUNNO WHAT YOU'RE DOING, BUT I'M--
--COACH, GIMME ANOTHER TEN TONS--
--I'M GOIN' FOR IT OVER HERE.
YES, SIR.
SURE, YOU ARE. "TEN TONS."
COACHBOT, HIT ME WITH ANOTHER FIFTEEN.
YES, MA'AM.
YOU AIN'T EVEN CLOSE TA CATCHIN' UP WITH ME YET.
COACH, GIMME ANOTHER TWENTY-FIVE.
YES, SIR.
WHEW! EIGHTY-FIVE TONS.
THAT'S IT FOR ME.
C'MON, JENNY--
--LAST ONE TO A HUNDRED TONS IS A DUMMY--

WHAT DID YOU CALL ME?
YOU--
--HEARD ME--
--"DUMMY."
OH, THAT'S IT--
POOR FORM! POOR FORM!
POOR FORM!
JEEZ!
NICE GIRL LIKE YOU OUGHTA--
--RRAAAAH--
--OUGHTA BE WATCHIN' HER FIGURE, BUT YOU'VE REALLY PACKED IT ON, HAVEN'TCHA?
BEN GRIMM, YOU WILL LIVE TO REGRET THAT--!
ATTENTION ALL FANTASTIC FOUR SENIOR STAFF. ATTENTION:
SENIOR STAFF TRANSITION CONFERENCE TO BE HELD IN THE OMEGA ROOM BEGINS IN FIFTEEN MINUTES.
ATTENDANCE IS MANDATORY.
AWWW.
AWWW.

WELCOME TO THE OMEGA ROOM.
WE USED TO HAVE A PANIC FLOOR, BUT WE UPGRADED.
HI. COME ON IN.
JENNIFER, THIS PLACE IS A KIND OF MAYDAY SUITE.
IT'S THE SAFEST PLACE IN THE UNIVERSE AND IF, FOR WHATEVER REASON, YOU OR THE KIDS NEED A SAFE FALLBACK POSITION, IT--
--YOU KNOW WHAT, THE TUTORIAL AND BUILDING INTRODUCTION WE'VE PREPARED WILL TELL YOU ALL ABOUT IT. FOR NOW, HOWEVER...
...FOR NOW, I WANTED EVERYONE TO HAVE THE CHANCE TO MEET ONE ANOTHER FACE-TO-FACE.
AH...

WE START--
--SORRY--
WE STARTING?
WHAT?
HAVE YOU FORGOTTEN TO DO SOMETHING IMPORTANT, JOHN?
OH, MAN--!

WHAT?
NO.
ARE YOU SERIOUS?
NO.
DARLA, PLEASE--
--PLEEEEEEEASE--
--PLEASE DO THIS THING FOR ME. PLEASE JOIN THE FANTASTIC FOUR IN MY PLACE.
DARLA, IT'S A STUNT. IT'S A--
HANG ON.
--IT'S A P.R. STUNT, IT'S FOUR MINUTES ON A TUESDAY MORNING AND--
JOHNNY, HANG ON--
THE WIG FEELS GREAT, JULIAN. I WANT TO MAKE SURE I CAN DANCE IN IT, BUT IT FEELS GREAT.
GOOD, GOOD.
THESE DUDES YOUR ROOMMATES?
JOHNNY, I'M KIND OF A BIG DEAL. LIKE, IN MUSIC. YOU KNOW THAT, RIGHT?
I HAVE A WORLD TOUR COMING UP IN SIX WEEKS. NINETEEN COUNTRIES, ONE HUNDRED AND FORTY VENUES, SIX STAGES, FIFTY COSTUME CHANGES?
I'VE TALKED ABOUT NOTHING BUT THIS, LITERALLY, FOR LIKE THE LAST SIX MONTHS.
DARLA. FOUR MINUTES NEXT TUESDAY MORNING...
COME WITH ME FOR A SEC.
LET ME SHOW YOU HOW AMAZING IT IS TO BE IN THE FANTASTIC FOUR, EVEN IF IT'S JUST FOR FOUR MINUTES, AND WHY YOU SHOULD TOTALLY DO THIS FOR ME.

IS THAT A MONKEY?
YES!
NO.
THIS APPEARS TO BE A MUTATED GENETIC OFFSHOOT OF HOMO HABILIS, A SWEETLY UNIQUE LITTLE CUL-DE-SAC ON THE WAY TO HOMO ERECTUS.
THE SUSPENSION TANK PRESERVES HIS LIFE AND PROTECTS HIM FROM AN ENVIRONMENT AND ECOSYSTEM THAT WOULD QUITE HONESTLY KILL HIM ON CONTACT.
WE WERE PLACING A CHRONAL ANCHOR ABOUT 2.66 MILLION YEARS AGO, GIVE OR TAKE, AND...WELL, SOMEONE WASN'T DOING THEIR JOB, AND WE ENDED UP ACCIDENTALLY SENDING HIM HERE.
HEY, I TOLD YOU GUYS THAT WAS NOT MY FAULT--
WOULD YOU CARE TO GO TO THE TAPE, MY FRIEND? I THINK YOU'LL FIND THAT A PICTURE IS WORTH A THOUSAND--
YOU'RE GOING TO SEND HIM BACK, RIGHT?
I MEAN, YOU HAVE TO SEND HIM BACK.
DON'T YOU?

TWO-POINT-SIX-SIX MILLION YEARS BEFORE NOW.
OoOOOOHH...
EASY THERE, DARLA, I GOT YOU.
OOK--
SPACE-TIME TRAVEL TAKES SOME GETTING USED TO.
YOU CAN GET USED TO THIS?
IT ALL TAKES SOME GETTING USED TO. BUT ONCE YOU DO?
ONCE YOU DO, THE STUFF YOU SEE JUST CAN'T BE BEAT.
OOK! OOOOOK!

BWWOOOARRRRKK!!
BOY, THIS MIGHT SOUND CRAZY, BUT I THINK THERE'S A CONNECTION BETWEEN THAT DINOSAUR AND OUR BUDDY THE--
OOK!
AAAIIIEEE!
AFTER...
AFTER ALL WE'VE DONE FOR THAT GUY.
OOK! OOK!
BWAAAAAARRRRR!!
JOHNNY--
YEAH, YEAH--

FLAME ON!
OOK! OOK!
COUPLE OF BROKEN RECORDS, THE BOTH OF YOU.
BWOOORRRGGKK!!
JOHNNY, THIS THING IS STARTING TO GLOW!
GO, GO--
--GO!

WOW.
BON VOYAGE!
THAT'S A THING PEOPLE SAY, RIGHT?
I DUNNO-- I GOT STRAIGHT D'S IN SPANISH, BABE.
C'MERE.
YOU'RE SURE SHE'S UP TO ALL THIS? I'M TRUSTING YOUR JUDGMENT HERE, JOHN.
SURE I'M SURE.
BESIDES, IT'S JUST GOING TO BE FOUR MINUTES FOR HER, RIGHT?
WHAT'S THE WORST THAT CAN HAPPEN?

WATCH OUT, FRANKLIN-- DON'T WANT TO PINCH YOU.
REMEMBER, VAL, IF YOU THINK YOU'RE GONNA BOOT, AIM IT AT UNCLE BEN, OKAY?
OKAY.
MAG ENGINES AT FULL CHARGE. WE'RE LOOKIN' GOOD FOR DEPARTURE SPEED.
ROGER THAT. ACTIVATING THE CHRONOSTELLAR MANIFOLD NOW.
COURSE LAID IN FOR CHRONOSTELLAR MANIFOLD. STANDIN' BY FOR ACTIVATION.
ARE WE THERE YET?
ARE WE THERE YET?
ARE WE THERE YET?
CHRONOSTELLAR MANIFOLD AT FULL POWER. THE WINDOW IS OPEN.
WE'RE READY IN 10...9...8... 7...6...5...
"4...
"3...
"2...
"1."
IGNITION.

YAAAAAAAA-HOO!!!
SORRY, FOLKS.
BEEN A WHILE.
"NO WORRIES, BEN. I THINK WE'RE ALL FEELING IT.
"WE'VE JUST PASSED OUR LAST OPPORTUNITY TO DITCH, BY THE WAY.
"CHRONALTEMPORAL DEPARTURE IS IMMINENT IN 3...2...
"1."

WOW.
THERE'S SOMETHING YOU DON'T SEE EVERY DAY.
WELL, FOLKS, THERE IT IS.
FOR THE NEXT TWO HUNDRED AND FORTY SECONDS, WE'RE THE FANTASTIC FOUR.
TWO-THIRTY.
TWO-TWENTY-FIVE.
SO FAR SO GOOD, RIGHT?
RIGHT.
THIS IS GOING GREAT.
BE OVER BEFORE WE KNOW IT.

"WE WON'T EVEN KNOW THEY'RE GONE."

FF #2 — “THE BIG GOODBYE”

4 DAY ONE:
I'LL BE BACK BEFORE YOU CAN TWEET I LEFT.
STAY GORGEOUS.
FOUR MINUTES?
ONLY FOUR MINUTES.
WOW.
LADIES AND GENTLEMEN, FOR THE NEXT TWO HUNDRED AND FORTY SECONDS--
WE ARE THE FANTASTIC FOUR.

THIS IS GOING *GREAT.*
BE OVER BEFORE WE KNOW IT.

YOU HOLDING IT TOGETHER OVER THERE, SCOTT?
YEP.
YEP YEP YEP.

UH-OH.
DON'T SAY "UH-OH."
WHY DID YOU SAY "UH-OH"?
12
11

UH-OH.

"MR. LANG?
LATE CITY FINAL
DAILY BUGLE
ANT-ASTIC FOUR?
REPLACEMENTS SHUN SPOTLIGHT
RICHARDS FAMILY MISSING IN TIME AND SPACE
"WHAT IS AN 'EX-CON'?"
AH--EXCUSE ME, ONOME?
AN "EX-CON"? IT SAYS HERE THAT YOU'RE, QUOTE--
" --AN EX-CON WITH DELUSIONS OF SUPER-HEROIC GRANDEUR."
WOW--
DAY TWO:
IT MEANS, UH--
--LOOK, KIDS, LIFE IS LONG AND THE ROAD YOU--
--SOMETIMES WHEN A MAN--
--IT MEANS I DON'T KNOW WHAT IT MEANS?
IT MEANS HE'S BEEN CONVICTED OF A CRIME.
AND NOW HE'S RUNNING BOTH THE FANTASTIC FOUR AND THE FUTURE FOUNDATION.
IT COULD MEAN THAT, YES.

HEN I WAS
'OUNGER...
...I MADE MISTAKES. AND I PAID THE PRICE FOR IEM AND PUT MYSELF ON THE TRAIGHT AND NARROW, AND AVE ACTUALLY MANAGED TO NOT BREAK TOO MANY LAWS SUBSEQUENTLY.
REED KNEW THIS. EVERYBODY KNOWS THIS.
WE DIDN'T KNOW.
WELL, NOW YOU DO. I USED TO STEAL THINGS. LOOK--
--DON'T LET THE NEWSPAPER OR ANYTHING ELSE YOU HEAR GET YOU RILED UP. REED AND THOSE GUYS--
--THEY'RE ALL FINE. WE'LL BE FINE. I DON'T KNOW WHY THEY DIDN'T COME BACK WHEN THEY THOUGHT THEY WOULD, BUT THEY WILL. THEY'RE FINE. I KNOW IT.
YOU CANNOT KNOW IT. AND YET YOU SOUND SURE.
HOW IS IT THAT YOU SOUND SO SURE OF YOURSELF?
A SUPER HERO! WE ALL ARE. AND WHILE WE MAY NOT BE THE FANTASTIC FOUR--
--I BELIEVE IN US. WE'LL BE FINE. ALL WE HAVE TO DO IS HOLD TIGHT AND HOLD TOGETHER. OKAY?
SPEAKING OF...
"...WHERE'S MEDUSA?"
ERM.
HELLO?
TING TING
EH, MAYBE SHE'S SLEEPING IN. SHE'S FINE.
EVERYTHING'S FINE.
MAYBE NOBODY LEAVE THE BUILDING TODAY.

DAY THREE:
MS. DARLA...?
GOOD MORNING, GUYS.
YOU PANCAKE.
THEY GONED.
'SCUSE.
DOES THAT MEAN SOMEBODY ALREADY *ATE* MY PANCAKES?
NO.
yes
LOOKING AT?
SKY?
SEE THE CHRONO...FOLD... THINGY UP THERE? THAT.
THE THING THE FANTASTIC FOUR ARE SUPPOSED TO COME THROUGH AGAIN SOME DAY. AND TRYING NOT TO FEEL COMPLETELY *USELESS.*
MACHINE.
SAYS "BOOP BOOP."
HAS ROOM.
COME SEE.

4 MACHINE THAT SAYS "BOOP BOOP" ROOM:
...WOW.
GOOD MORNING, MR... AH--
MR. MAN?
DRAGON MAN IS FINE, MS. DEERING, AND GOOD MORNING.
THE REST OF THE FUTURE FOUNDATION IS ATTENDING A LECTURE BY MS. WALTERS--

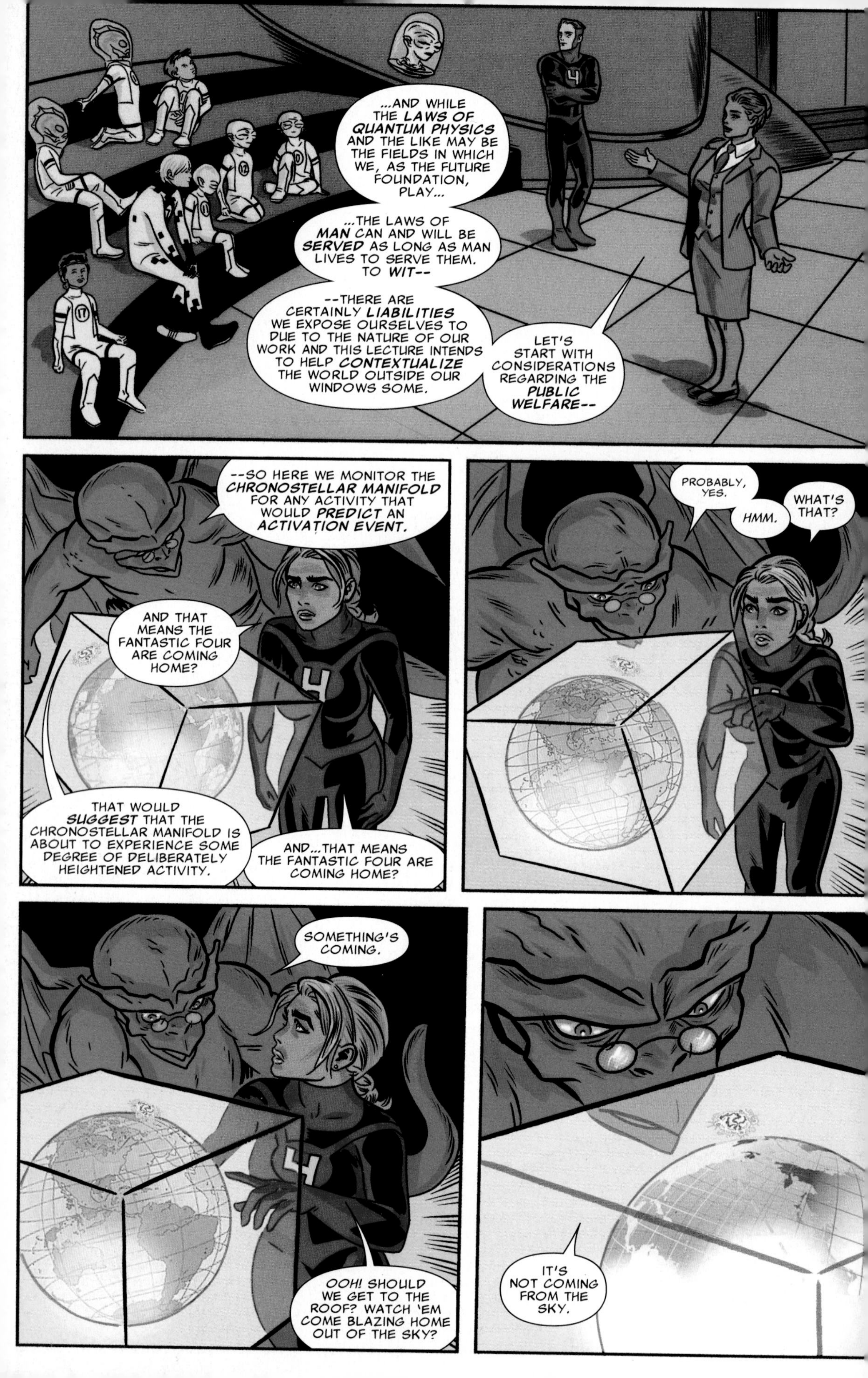
...AND WHILE THE LAWS OF QUANTUM PHYSICS AND THE LIKE MAY BE THE FIELDS IN WHICH WE, AS THE FUTURE FOUNDATION, PLAY...
...THE LAWS OF MAN CAN AND WILL BE SERVED AS LONG AS MAN LIVES TO SERVE THEM. TO WIT--
--THERE ARE CERTAINLY LIABILITIES WE EXPOSE OURSELVES TO DUE TO THE NATURE OF OUR WORK AND THIS LECTURE INTENDS TO HELP CONTEXTUALIZE THE WORLD OUTSIDE OUR WINDOWS SOME.
LET'S START WITH CONSIDERATIONS REGARDING THE PUBLIC WELFARE--
--SO HERE WE MONITOR THE CHRONOSTELLAR MANIFOLD FOR ANY ACTIVITY THAT WOULD PREDICT AN ACTIVATION EVENT.
AND THAT MEANS THE FANTASTIC FOUR ARE COMING HOME?
THAT WOULD SUGGEST THAT THE CHRONOSTELLAR MANIFOLD IS ABOUT TO EXPERIENCE SOME DEGREE OF DELIBERATELY HEIGHTENED ACTIVITY.
AND...THAT MEANS THE FANTASTIC FOUR ARE COMING HOME?
PROBABLY, YES.
HMM.
WHAT'S THAT?
SOMETHING'S COMING.
OOH! SHOULD WE GET TO THE ROOF? WATCH 'EM COME BLAZING HOME OUT OF THE SKY?
IT'S NOT COMING FROM THE SKY.

IMPOSTORS!
YOU DARE CALL YOURSELVES THE FANTASTIC FOUR?!
NONSENSE!
FOOM
YOU GOTTA BE KIDDING ME...

YOU KNOW HOW HARD IT WAS TO GET A STELLA McCARTNEY IN MY SIZE?
YOU RUIN THIS AND I'M GOING TO WEAR YOU FOR SHOES, MOLE MAN.
YOU DARE--?
THERE ARE CHILDREN HERE, FIEND.
"FIEND"! THAT'S RIGHT-- FIEND! MONSTER! TERROR!
I AM THE GREATEST FOE THE FANTASTIC FOUR EVER FACED, AND YOU ARE CHEAP IMITATIONS!
MS. DEERING, TECHNICALLY YOU ARE A MEMBER OF THE FANTASTIC FOUR.
WE NEED TO GET YOU OUT THERE.
UM.
NO?

MEDUSA, CIVILIANS.
SHE-HULK, HEAVY ARTILLERY.
I GOT THE LITTLE GUY.
THIS OBSCENE MASQUERADE OF YOURS SHALL NOT STAND!
BOO.
OW! MY EYE!
KRAKK

WAIT.
HERE.
AAOOW!
ZORP
AAA--
RUN VERY FAR AND VERY FAST AWAY FROM HERE.

AH, STELLA.
PARTING IS SUCH SWEET SORROW.
MOLE MAN IS DOWN, LADIES.
HIS PET IS NEXT--!
WE ARE NOT AMUSED.
WHAT IS THIS THING?
WELL, YOU SEE, ONCE UPON A TIME, MR. GRIMM FOUND HIMSELF TRANSFORMED TO HIS HUMAN STATE WITH NO HOPE OF BECOMING THE ROCKY THING AGAIN, OR SO HE THOUGHT, WHEN DR. RICHARDS BUILT--
AR

STRONG--
--IT'S TOO STRONG--
WHOA--
--WATCH OUT, WATCH OUT--
WHAMMO
GGRRRAAAH--!
WATCH OUT, SCOTT. WHEREVER YOU ARE--
A LITTLE WARNING BEFORE THE HIT NEXT TIME--!

NYARGH*
NKT
*THIS WAS SUPPOSED TO BE MY DAY OFF! --translated from Gigantese.
...WOW, YOU GUYS.
SNAP
HOT-DIGITTY DOG, WOTTA SCOOP!
HEY, FANTASTIC FOUR--
PRESS
--SAY CHEESE--

DAY FOUR:
DAILY BUGLE
CITY TO FANTASTIC FOUR
PAY UP!!
WELL, AT LEAST THEY DIDN'T GO WITH "ANT-ASTIC" AGAIN.
THAT'S A TERRIBLE PICTURE OF ME.
NO SUCH THING AS BAD PRESS, MEDUSA--
--VIL, STOP STABBING WU'S HAND, PLEASE.
UM, GUYS...?
THIS WAS A REALLY BAD DECISION. I DON'T KNOW WHAT I'M DOING HERE.
I WANT TO GO HOME. OKAY?
I THINK I'M GOING TO GO HOME.

BUT...
BUT YOU CAN'T?
SCOTT.
I'M GOING TO GET SOMEBODY HURT. MAYBE EVEN KILLED. I HAVE NO BUSINESS BEING IN THIS WORLD. ESPECIALLY IF THE FANTASTIC FOUR--
--THE REAL FANTASTIC FOUR--
--ARE JUST GONE.
YOU SHOULD FIND SOMEONE ELSE. I'M SORRY.
I'M SO SORRY.
YEAH, BACK TO THE SAME-O, SAME-O, OF GLOBAL POP-MEGASTARDOM FOR YOU, LITTLE MISSY.
AAAAAAUUGH, I COULD REALLY USE SOME GOOD NEWS RIGHT NOW--
BOOP BOOP BOOP BOOP
THE MACHINE THAT SAYS "BOOP BOOP"...

BOOP BOOP BOOP BOOP
ANYBODY SEE THEM?
ANYBODY SEE ANYTHING YET?
THERE.
ANYBODY KNOW WHERE THE LITTLE GOLD NAKED GUYS ARE?
SLEEPING IN A DITCH. WHO CARES?

WAIT.
SOMETHING'S WRONG.
I'M ALIVE!
I'M ALIVE...

SHOOOSH
WHAT IS HE DOING? WHERE IS THE VESSEL?
NO... NO NO NO...
I'M ALIVE!
YOU DIDN'T KILL ME TODAY!
ZISSK
FZAK
AND YOU WON'T KILL ME TOMORROW!
HE'S INSANE. AND HE'S--
HE'S COMING TOWARDS US.
WHROOMM
I LIVE!
AND NOW...

THE FANTASTIC FOUR ARE DEAD!
AND NO ONE CAN EVER GO THROUGH THAT GATEWAY AGAIN...

FF #3 — "OLD JOHN STORM"

MY NAME IS JOHN STORM. YOU KNEW ME AS THE HUMAN TORCH.
THE FANTASTIC FOUR DIED BEYOND THE VEIL OF SPACE AND TIME. I ESCAPED TO MAKE SURE THE EVIL THAT HUNTED MY FAMILY LIKE ANIMALS ACROSS INFINITE TIME AND SPACE DIES HERE AND NOW.
SO... WHAT'S NEXT?
KIDS.
GO TO BED.
IT'S 4:30 AND I'M NINETEEN AND IT'S NEW YEAR'S.
THEN GO FIND THE MOLOIDS, ALEX.
NO.
FINE.
JOHNNY. JOHN--
--HOW?

FTAAK
"I RAN.
"FOR YEARS, I RAN, TRYING TO FIND A WAY HOME. TRYING TO ESCAPE...

"DOOM.
"THE ANNIHILATING CONQUEROR.
FZZAK
FZZAK
"VICTOR VON DOOM. KANG THE CONQUEROR. AND AN ANNIHILUS KANG HAD PLUCKED FROM TIME.
"THE THREE OF THEM CAME TOGETHER AND FORMED AN UNHOLY ALLIANCE.
"THEY JOINED FORCES-- THEY JOINED FORMS-- TO TAKE ADVANTAGE OF THE FANTASTIC FOUR'S DEPARTURE FROM SPACE-TIME."
IT WAS A MASSACRE.
NO OTHER WORD FOR IT.
OTHER THAN "DOOM."

SIIICK.
MY... GOODNESS.
GOODNESS GOT NOTHIN' TO DO WITH IT.
OOOPH.
I CLOSED THE DOOR BEHIND ME, BUT BELIEVE ME--DOOM THE ANNIHILATING CONQUEROR WILL FIND HIS WAY THROUGH.
HE'LL KEEP HUNTING.
SO I SUPPOSE THE QUESTION I GOT FOR YOU IS...
WHAT ARE WE READY TO DO ABOUT DOOM?
YES, WELL.
...SCOTT?
WE NEED TO GET DARLA BACK, MEDUSA.
WE NEED TO FIGURE OUT WHO THIS GUY IS.
AND CAN SOMEBODY PLEASE FIND THE MOLOIDS? I GET WORRIED IF THEY'RE NOT UNDERFOOT.

4 ABOUT THOSE MOLOIDS:
WELL, THEN?
HAVE YOU BROUGHT THE MOLE MAN HIS TRIBUTE?
I HAVE UPHELD MY END OF THE BARGAIN.
AND RECEIVED SANCTION THUS FAR AS MY REWARD.
NOT EASY STEALING A STARHEART.
AND IT IS HEAVY!
WE THANK YOU FOR THE GIANT MESS YOU MADE FOR US. THE NEW FAMILY CAME TOGETHER GOOD AND FAST TO FIX IT.
DON'T TOUCH THE SPHERE. YOU'LL INCINERATE. FWOOF!
IN EXCHANGE, THEN. HERE. TAKE IT.
DON'T TELL US WHY YOU WANT IT. THAT WAY WE NEED NOT LIE WHEN YOU REQUIRE RESCUE.
WHICH YOU WILL. BECAUSE YOU ARE YOU, AND WE ARE US.

DO NOT CONTACT US AGAIN.
WAS THAT HARSH? THAT SOUNDED HARSH, MIK.
I HATE HIM, TONG. I DO NOT CARE.
I WOULD FILL THIS CHAMBER WITH MOLTEN STEEL IF I COULD.
TOO FAR, MIK.
MELTING STEEL!
HEY, BOYS...
SCOTT WAS--
--OOPH--
--LOOKING FOR YOU A BIT AGO.
THE JEN.
THE JENNNNNNNNNN.

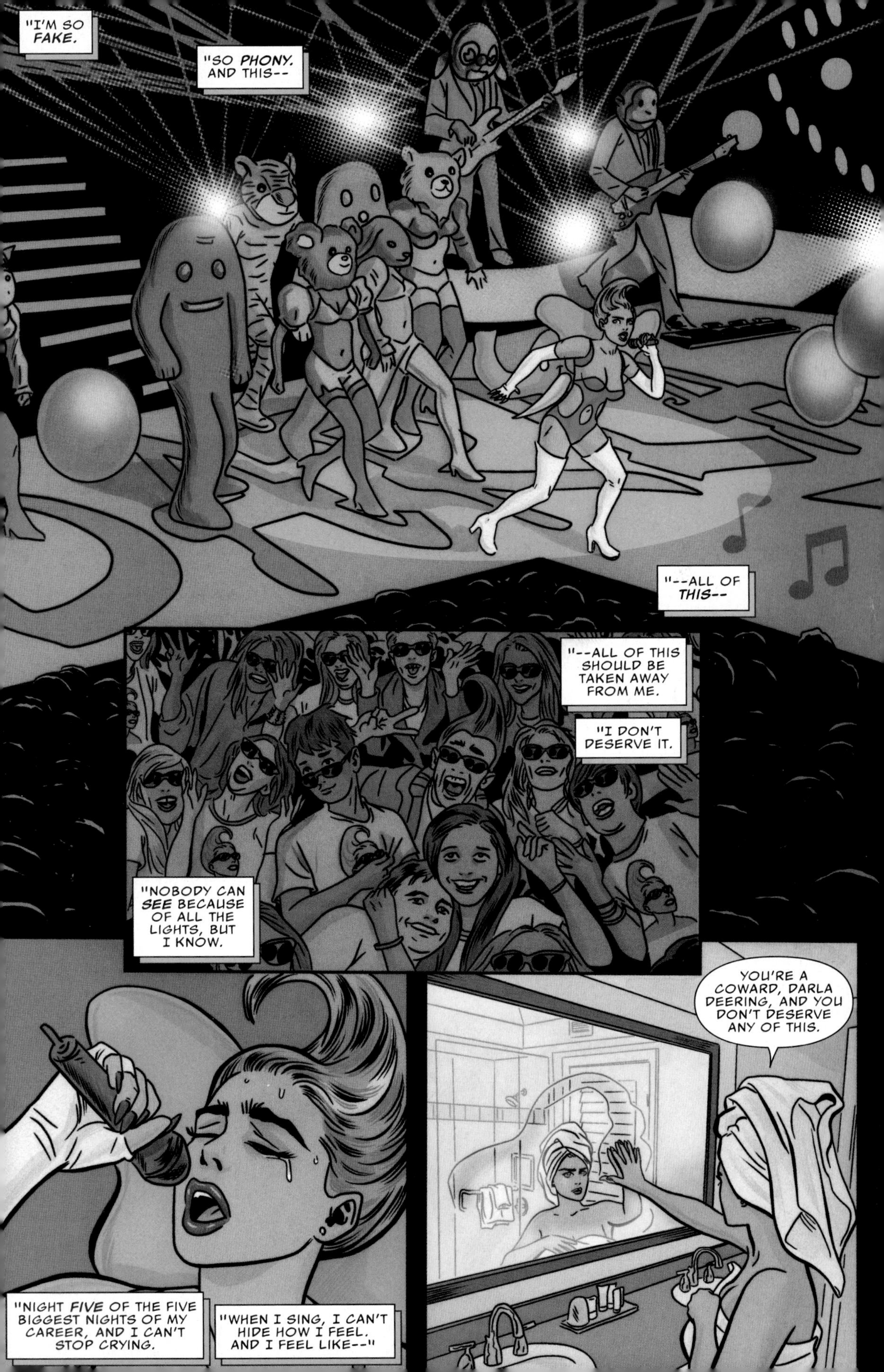
"I'M SO FAKE.
"SO PHONY. AND THIS--
"--ALL OF THIS--
"--ALL OF THIS SHOULD BE TAKEN AWAY FROM ME.
"I DON'T DESERVE IT.
"NOBODY CAN SEE BECAUSE OF ALL THE LIGHTS, BUT I KNOW.
"NIGHT FIVE OF THE FIVE BIGGEST NIGHTS OF MY CAREER, AND I CAN'T STOP CRYING.
"WHEN I SING, I CAN'T HIDE HOW I FEEL. AND I FEEL LIKE--"
YOU'RE A COWARD, DARLA DEERING, AND YOU DON'T DESERVE ANY OF THIS.

TCH.
WOW, WHO SPENT TWENTY WHOLE BUCKS ON...
OH BOY, SHE SAW 'EM, SHE SAW 'EM--
DARLA-
"THE TERRIFIC THREE" SOUNDS STUPID AND I DON'T WANT TO PAY FOR NEW UNIFORMS. COME BACK TO US.
-SCOTT
WAIT, IS SHE CRYING?
OH, DON'T BE CRYING, NOW I FEEL LIKE A CREEP...

KNOCK KNOCK
DELIVERY FOR YOU, MA'AM.
UM.
WHO'S IT FROM?
DUNNO, MA'AM.
WELL, DO I NEED TO SIGN FOR IT, OR--
OH.
WAIT, WHAT'S HAPPENING OUT THERE?
WHERE IS SHE? IS SHE--
WHAT THE--
WHAT'S A "YANCY STREET GANG"?

DARLA--!
SPLOOOOOSHH
BTAM
WHUZZ
I--
--SCOTT? WERE YOU--
WHAT JUST HAPPENED?

I WAS--
--I HAD THIS WHOLE THING PLANNED OUT IN MY HEAD, WITH THE FLOWERS, AND I WOULD--
WHAT JUST HAPPENED, SCOTT?
A DEVICE. A BOMB FULL OF...
FUDGE OR WHIPPED CREAM OR SOMETHING. I DON'T KNOW.
I FELT THE VIBRATIONS WHEN I WAS DOWNSCALED...
THERE WAS A NOTE. IT WAS SIGNED--
YANCY STREET SAYS HI, DUMMY!
YOU AIN'T NO KINDA THING, AND YOU AIN'T NO KINDA FANTASTIC FOUR!
WHAT... THE...
FF. WE'RE THE FF--
--AND YOU BETTER RUN!

MY BROTHER.
MY MAN.

I KNOW JOHNNY STORM AS I KNOW MY OWN FLESH AND BLOOD.
THIS MAN IS MY BROTHER.
AND YOU TRUST THIS WYATT WINGFOOT'S CHARACTER?
I DO.
AND YOU TRUST HIS ABILITY TO JUDGE CHARACTER?
I DO.
LITERALLY EVERY SINGLE PIECE OF MACHINERY REED RICHARDS LEFT BEHIND THAT COULD IDENTIFY JOHNNY STORM HAS IDENTIFIED THAT MAN AS HE.
EVEN THE FRONT DOORS.
WELL THEN, WE MUST ASSUME THREE THINGS. FIRST, SOMETHING HAS GONE VERY WRONG IN TIME AND SPACE WITH THE FANTASTIC FOUR.
SECOND, THEY ARE NOT COMING BACK.
AND THIRD, ANY HOPE WE HAVE IN SAVING THEM LIES WITH THAT MAN IN THERE WHO QUITE FRANKLY MIGHT BE INSANE.

YANCY STREEEEEET!
DARLA, COME ON--
SCOTT, THEY MIGHT BE DANGEROUS, WE DON'T KNOW WHO THEY ARE--
SURE WE DO. THEY'RE JERKS.
THEY'RE INTERNET JERKS COME ON!
YANCY STREEEEEET!
EXIT
BMP

WAIT, SCOTT, WE--

PSHT.

HOLD THE ELEVATOR, PLEASE...
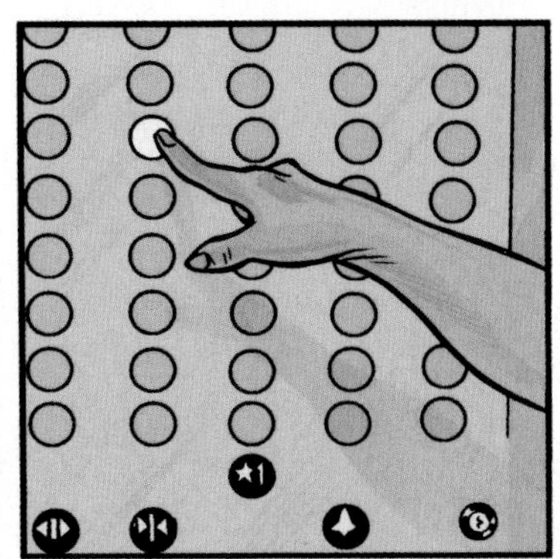

ZOM
HAAAUUGH... HHAAUFF.
C'MON, GUYS-- ALMOST--
INTERNET JERKS!
I-- THAT--
I--
I KNOW. PRETTY AMAZING, RIGHT? EXPRESS ELEVATOR.
I'M HAVING A HEART ATTACK.
WUMP
WE GOTTA GET THE LAST ONE BEFORE HE GETS OUTSIDE--
--OR THOSE PICTURES'LL BE POSTED ON STALKER BEFORE BREAKFAST--
C'MON, OLD MAN--
--HEART--
--ATTACK--
--SERIOUSLY--
WHITT
OH, NO--
--OH, NO--

Broadway
HAPPY NEW YEAR!
NEW YEAR'S...
DARLA...

LOST HIM.
YEAH, THERE'S A BILLION AND FIFTY PEOPLE OUT HERE. HE'S GONE.
BUT, DARLA, LOOK...
THEY'RE GONE. THEY'RE NOT COMING BACK.
SOMETHING HAPPENED OUT THERE TO THEM, DARLA, AND THEY'RE NOT COMING BACK.
NOT THE JERKS. I MEAN THEM.
I DON'T...
SOMETHING HAPPENED TO THE FANTASTIC FOUR?
YEAH. I DON'T KNOW WHAT.
THAT'S NOT TRUE. I KNOW EXACTLY WHAT.
THEN, WHAT?
WE WERE THEIR LAST WISHES, DARLA. THE FOUR OF US. NOT THREE AND SOME RINGER, NOT TWO-AND-TWO, NOT ME AND THREE AVENGERS.
US. I KNOW IT'S SCARY. I KNOW IT'S NEW.
DANGEROUS. BUT--
NO, I KNOW. I KNOW. YOU'RE RIGHT.
WHAT ARE...WHAT ARE WE GONNA DO NOW?

WE'RE GOING TO END DOOM.
WHAT?

LADIES AND GENTLEMEN:
I PROPOSE DIRECTING THE ENERGIES OF THE FUTURE FOUNDATION TO RESOLVING ONE OF THE ENDURING ISSUES THAT STANDS IN THE WAY OF EARTH'S ONGOING AND SAFE DEVELOPMENT.
LET'S END DOOM.
ONCE AND FOR ALL. FOREVER.
I WANT US TO ERADICATE THE VERY THOUGHT OF DOOM FROM HUMAN EXISTENCE.
NOW THAT...
THAT IS A GREAT IDEA, LITTLE MAN...

FANTASTIC FOUR #3 — "FIRST BOOTS ON THE GROUND"

DATE ON EARTH: 01.01.13
DISTANCE FROM EARTH: 37.984 LIGHT-YEARS
SSSSSSSIGH.
HAPPY NEW YEAR, BENJY-BOY.
AR

RATE OF MY MOLECULAR DECAY SEEMS SLOW YET STEADY.
THIS THING THAT'S KILLING ME IS STILL DOING ITS WORK. WE ARE THIRTY-EIGHT LIGHT-YEARS AWAY FROM HOME.
ONG-RANGE SCANS HAVE INDICATED SOMETHING INTERESTING ABOUT ZETA DORADUS.
IT'S NOT CARBON-BASED AT ALL BUT RATHER...WELL, IT WOULD APPEAR TO BE A VIRGIN WORLD FORMED OF SOMETHING ENTIRELY UNSTABLE.
THE NATURAL DECAY OF THE UNSTABLE MOLECULES THAT MAKE THINGS LIKE OUR UNIFORMS POSSIBLE MATCHES THE DECAY RATE OF MY OWN CELLS.
TO BE ABLE TO STUDY A NATURALLY OCCURRING QUANTUM MOLECULE, INCHOATE AND RAW-- TO STUDY AN UNSTABLE MOLECULE IN THE VERY HOUR OF ITS BIRTH...
...WELL, I KNOW HOW THE STORY ENDS. MAYBE I CAN LEARN MORE ABOUT HOW IT BEGAN.
MY...I'M HESITANT TO CALL IT A LIE, EVEN IF THE CASE CAN BE MADE IT'S A LIE OF OMISSION.
MY COVER FOR COMING TO THIS DISTANT PLACE IS THAT IT'S BARELY BEEN SEEN, LET ALONE STEPPED UPON BY ANYONE...
WE DESCEND AT DAWN. IT'LL BE FUN FOR THE--
DAD!
SPEAK OF THE DEVIL, AND THE DEVIL APPEARS.
THE DEVIL LIKE DIABLO?
NO, YOU GOON, IT'S JUST AN EXPRESSION.

WELL, WELL, MY LITTLE ASTRONAUTS. TO WHAT DO I OWE THE PLEASURE?
THE PLANET, DAD.
WE'RE HERE. ZETA DORITO.
DORADUS.
I SUPPOSE YOU CAN NAME IT WHATEVER YOU LIKE.
JOHNNY, THAT'S SPECIALLY CALIBRATED TO SUPPORT BEN'S WEIGHT IN THE SIMULATED GRAVITY OF THE SHIP...
NO DUH, DOCTOR PHIL. THAT'S THE POINT.
THIRTY-EIGHT LIGHT-YEARS AWAY FROM EARTH AND SOME THINGS REFUSE TO CHANGE...
DADDY.
WHO GETS TO WALK ON THE PLANET FIRST?
ERM--
LADIES FIRST, DADDY.
WHY SHOULDN'T I BE THE FIRST ONE TO WALK ON THE NEW PLANET?
I, AH, I--
NO. DAD. COME ON.
DAD. IT'S ME. RIGHT? RIGHT?
SUSAN!
I'M IN THE COCKPIT, DEAR.
EVERYBODY MIGHT WANT TO COME SEE THIS.

ZETA DORADUS:
WE'RE HERE.
SEE?
WOWWWWW.
THERE NOW. HOW GREAT IS THAT?
PRETTY GREAT. GOTTA SAY.
BEN, COULD YOU JOIN US IN THE COCKPIT, PLEASE?
WE'VE ARRIVED.
YEAH, YEAH.
HURRAH FOR BEIN' FIRST BOOTS ON THE GROUND.

"ATMOSPHERIC PRESSURE DOWN THERE IS QUITE PROMISING, BUT THE ATMOSPHERE ITSELF IS KIND OF LIKE SOUP.
"WHAT WE'RE DOING IS LAUNCHING A KIND OF OXYGEN HARVESTER DOWN THERE. IT'LL SUCK THE SOUP IN AND ALTER IT INTO SOMETHING MORE COMFORTABLE FOR HUMANS.
"WE'LL BE ABLE TO SE BETTER AND SOUND WI CARRY BETTER IN ITS OPERATING RADIUS.
"WE'LL SUIT UP AND TAKE TH BOAT DOWN TO THE SURFACE.
"WE'LL LAND NEAR THE HARVESTER. MOM WILL BE READY TO DOME THINGS OFF IF NEED BE.
"WE'LL SPEND THE MORNING AND COME BACK BEFORE LUNCH.
"I'LL EXPECT YOU BOTH TO COLLECT SOIL SAMPLES FOR ANALYSIS AND PHOTOGRAPHIC DOCUMENTATION FOR YOUR REPORTS, NATURALLY."
ANY QUESTIONS?
YEAH.
WHAT'S WRONG WITH UNCLE BEN?
NOTHING. HE'S A ROCK.

"HE'LL BE FINE.
"EVERYTHING'S GOING TO BE FINE."
SHUTTLE TO BEN--WE'LL BE BACK BY LUNCHTIME.
GOTCHA, STRETCHO.
DO MY BEST TO KEEP IT QUIET UP HERE WHILE YOU'RE GONE.
GO HAVE YERSELVES AN ADVENTURE DOWN THERE.

ARE WE THERE YET?
ARE WE THERE YET?
ARE WE THERE YET?
ARE WE THERE YET?
ARE WE THERE YET?
JONATHAN LOWELL SPENCER STORM, DO NOT MAKE ME TURN THIS SHUTTLE AROUND.
WE'LL BE TOUCHING DOWN IN A MINUTE.
WHO GOES FIRST?
ONETWOTHREE*SHOOT!*
THAT...WOULD APPEAR TO BE NOT ROCK, NOR SCISSORS, NOR PAPER. WHAT IS THAT?
NULLIFIER.
SO WHO WON?

I DON'T UNDERSTAND. WHERE'S THE HARVESTER? WE FOLLOWED THE BEACON AND THERE SHOULD BE BREATHABLE AIR OUT HERE, BUT--
REED. WATCH THIS.
ONE...
TWO...
THREE!
WELL, THAT WAS ONE GIANT LEAP FOR ALL INVOLVED.
THANK GOD THEY DIDN'T BREAK THEIR ANKLES OUT HERE...
SUSAN.
WHERE IS OUR HARVESTER, AND WHY IS IT STILL BROADCASTING?
NOW THE BEACON'S STOPPED ENTIRELY. DID WE LAND ON TOP OF THE THING, OR--

WHOA.
MY WORD.
MOMMMMM!
OH, NO--

GET THE CHILDREN BACK TO THE SHIP--
JOHNNY, DON'T BE RIDICULOUS. THERE'S NOW OXYGEN, AND THE MIX THAT'S OUT THERE COULD MAKE THE ATMOSPHERE IGNITE.
WHOA-- YEAH--
--YEAH, RIGHT, JUST A FORCE OF HABIT SOMETIMES--
GET INSIDE, AND GET US READY TO RETURN TO THE SHIP.
WAY AHEAD OF YOU, STRETCH.
FLAME--
FRANK, VAL, HOLD ON--
MOMMY'S COMING--
MOMMMMMMM!
DADDDYYYYY!
KIDS.

WHOA, COOL--
JOHNNY...
GUYS'RE GONNA HAVE TO MAKE A RUN FOR IT.
THOSE THINGS ARE EVERYWHERE, AND IF I DON'T GET US OFF THE SURFACE--
JOHNNY.
JOHNNY!

MY WORD...
EASY, REED.
I'VE GOT THIS...
MY BIG SISTER.
HEAVY, REED.
IT'S VERY HEAVY.
I KNOW, MY DARLING, I KNOW.

REED, SHE CAN'T KEEP THIS GOING LONG.
I KNOW, JOHNNY, I KNOW...
MOMMY--?
MOMMY NEEDS TO CONCENTRATE, VAL.
SHE'S THE ONLY THING KEEPING US ALL ALIVE RIGHT NOW.
AHH, BEN?
BEN, WE'VE HAD A BIT OF A SITUATION DOWN HERE, AND THE WHOLE DAY'S GONE PEAR-SHAPED...
...BEN?
WRITE DOWN THE DAY AN' TIME YOU SAID THAT, STRETCH.

YOU AIN'T EVEN SEEN PEAR-SHAPED YET.

WELL, WHAT STARTED OFF AS A MISSION ABOUT EXPLORATION AND THE PIONEER SPIRIT IS RATHER EVOLVING ON THE FLY.
IT'S NOW ABOUT SURVIVAL, AND DARWINISM, AND MAYBE ABOUT NOT RUNNING OFF HALF-COCKED WHEN ONE FINDS SOMETHING EXCITING, SCIENTIFICALLY SPEAKING.
A PARTICULAR WEAK SPOT OF MY OWN, I ADMIT.
SO, NOW THEN. WHAT ARE OUR OPTIONS?
CAN WE COMMUNICATE WITH IT?
TOO LATE FOR THAT NOW-- IT'S TRYING TO KIL US. EAT US. WHATEVER.
WELL, THERE'S GOT TO BE SOME KIND OF INTELLIGENCE WE CAN REACH OUT TO.
I DON'T SEE ANY EARS OUT THERE. WE NEED TO RUN FOR IT.
THIS IS HOW WE INTRODUCE OURSELVES TO A NEW SPECIES? WE SHOW UP AND PUNCH IT REALLY HARD?
THEM OR US, VAL.
THEM OR US.
YEAH. YEAH, OKAY.
SO...HOW? MOM DROPS THE SHIELD AND WE'RE WORM FOOD.
WE'RE GOING TO NEED A FEW SECONDS TO GET THE SHUTTLE'S ENGINES UP.
UNCLE BEN?

WELL, BENJY-BOY.
YA MIGHT AS WELL LIVE.
ALL RIGHT, FANTASTIC FAMILY.
INCOMING.
WAIT FOR IT...
WAIT FOR IT...
THERE!
SO I'M LANDING AND JUST HITTIN' STUFF?
YOU'LL SEE, UNCLE BEN--
AND WHEN YOU DO...
...HIT HARD.

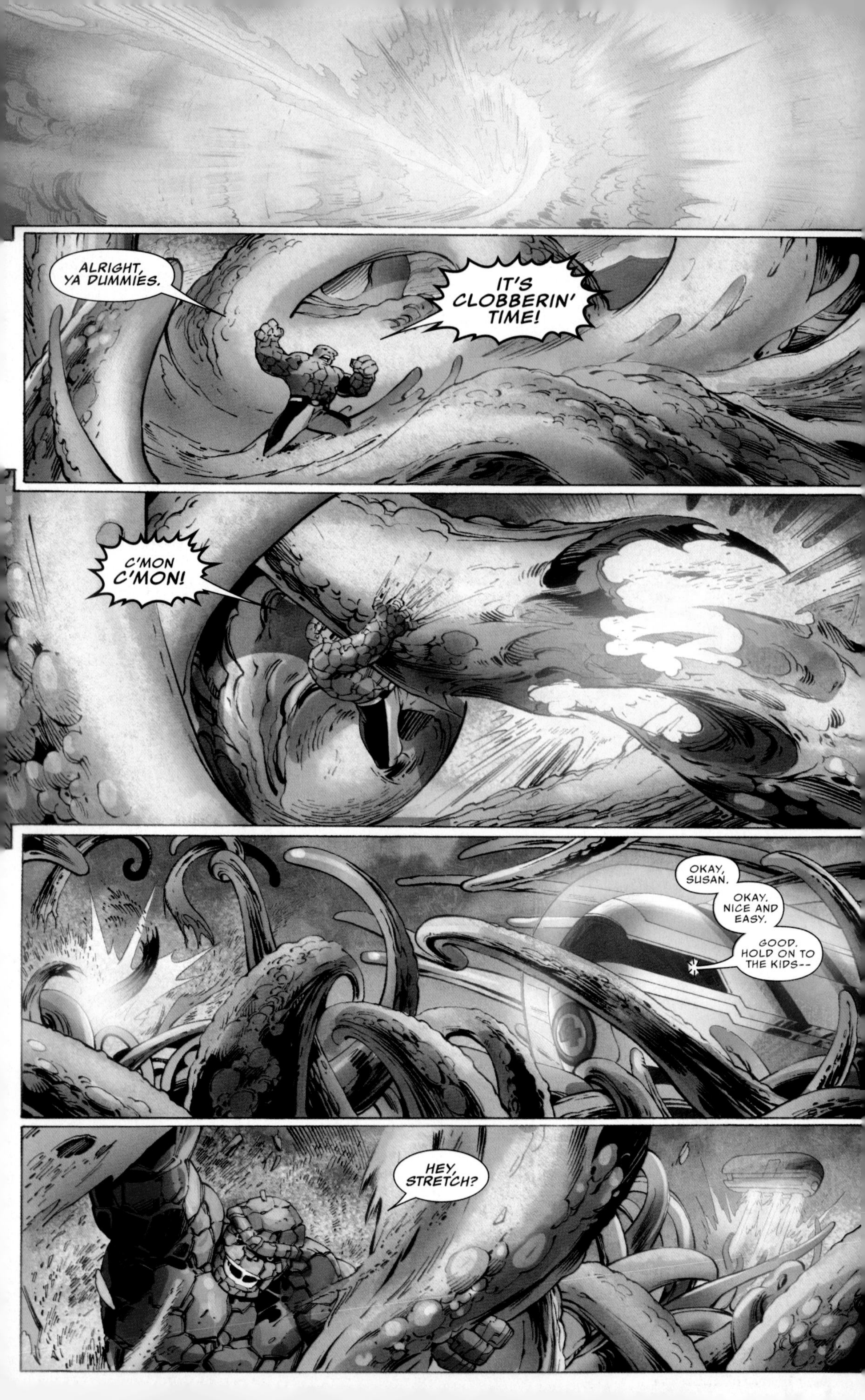

ALRIGHT, YA DUMMIES.
IT'S CLOBBERIN' TIME!
C'MON C'MON!
OKAY, SUSAN.
OKAY. NICE AND EASY.
GOOD. HOLD ON TO THE KIDS--
HEY, STRETCH?

HOW MUCH LONGER AM I KEEPIN' THIS UP?
WE'RE COMING TO GET YOU NOW.
STAY SHARP, IT'S GETTING HAIRY OUT HERE.
HAR DEE HAR HAR.
ANY TIME YOU DUMMIES WANNA COME PLAY CAVALRY, I'D APPRECIATE IT.
SUSAN.
CAN YOU DO THIS?
I CAN DO THIS. HANG ON, KIDS.
OKAY, JOHN.
I DON'T KNOW HOW LONG I CAN HOLD MY BREATH, REED, SO BE FAST.
FLAME ON!

COME ON COME ON COME ON COME ON--
GRRAAAHH!!
WHO'S NEXT, DUMMIES--?
STAND DOWN, BEN.
I THINK WE GOT OUR MESSAGE ACROSS...

HOW FASCINATING. ZETA DORADUS IS A KIND OF PLANETARY LURE FOR THAT COSMIC PREDATOR. LIKE THE VIPERFISH OR FIREFLY SQUID ON EARTH...
STAR-SIZED CONSCIOUSNESS. AMAZING.
WELL, BETWEEN BEING EATEN BY THAT THING, AND HAVING TO FIGHT OUR WAY OUT FROM INSIDE...
...I'M LAYING DOWN A NEW MOM RULE:
THIS IS THE LAST TIME SOMETHING LIKE THAT HAPPENS ON OUR TRIP.
YES, DEAR. OF COURSE.
"LESS ACTION, MORE ADVENTURE," YOU SAID. AND SO IT SHALL BE.
ABSOLUTELY. THE SAFETY OF THE CHILDREN IS OF PARAMOUNT IMPORTANCE.
'S NEW YEAR'S DAY. Y'KNOW? ON EARTH.
HAPPY NEW YEAR, YOU GUYS.
WELL THEN. HERE'S A RESOLUTION:
HERE'S TO A LOVELY, QUIET YEAR WITH NO MORE SURPRISES.
YES.
YES, OF COURSE.
HERE'S TO NO MORE UGLY SURPRISES.
NEXT: AN UGLY SURPRISE!

FANTASTIC FOUR #1 & FF #1 COMBINED VARIANTS

BY MARK BAGLEY, MARK FARMER & PAUL MOUNTS

FANTASTIC FOUR #1 VARIANT
BY DAVE JOHNSON

FANTASTIC FOUR #1 BABY VARIANT
BY SKOTTIE YOUNG

FANTASTIC FOUR #1 VARIANT
BY JOE QUESADA, DANNY MIKI & RICHARD ISANOVE

FANTASTIC FOUR #1 SKETCH VARIANT
BY JOE QUESADA & DANNY MIKI

FANTASTIC FOUR #1 PHANTOM VARIANT
BY C.P. WILSON

FANTASTIC FOUR #2 VARIANT
BY ADAM KUBERT & LAURA MARTIN

FANTASTIC FOUR #3 VARIANT
BY GABRIELE DELL'OTTO

FF #1 VARIANT
BY ARTHUR ADAMS & JUSTIN PONSOR

FF #1 BABY VARIANT
BY SKOTTIE YOUNG

FF #2 VARIANT
BY MICHAEL & LAURA ALLRED

FF #3 VARIANT
BY MICHAEL & LAURA ALLRED

THE FREE *MARVEL AUGMENTED REALITY APP* ENHANCES AND CHANGES THE WAY YOU EXPERIENCE COMICS!

To access the Marvel Augmented Reality App...

- **Download the app for free via marvel.com/ARapp**
- **Launch the app on your camera-enabled Apple iOS® or Android™ device***
- **Hold your mobile device's camera over any cover or panel with the AR graphic.**
- **Sit back and see the future of comics in action!**

*Available on most camera-enabled Apple iOS® and Android™ devices. Content subject to change and availability.

THE WORLD'S GREATEST COMIC MAGAZINE!

FANTASTIC FOUR

AR INDEX